WINSTON SPENCER CHURCHILL

SERVANT OF CROWN AND COMMONWEALTH

Toni Frissell

WINSTON SPENCER
CHURCHILL

SERVANT OF CROWN AND COMMONWEALTH

A TRIBUTE BY VARIOUS HANDS
PRESENTED TO HIM ON HIS
EIGHTIETH BIRTHDAY

EDITED BY

SIR JAMES MARCHANT
K.B.E.

with a portrait frontispiece

CASSELL & COMPANY LTD. LONDON

CASSELL & CO LTD.
37/38 St. Andrews Hill, Queen Victoria Street,
London, E.C.4.

and at

31/34 George IV Bridge, Edinburgh
210 Queen Street, Melbourne
26/30 Clarence Street, Sydney
Uhlmann Road, Hawthorne, Brisbane
C.P.O. 3031, Auckland, N.Z.
1068 Broadview Avenue, Toronto 6
P.O. Box 275, Cape Town
P.O. Box 1386, Salisbury, S. Rhodesia
P.O. Box 959, Accra, Gold Coast
122 East 55th Street, New York, 22
Avenida 9 de Julho 1138, São Paulo
Galeria Güemes, Escritorio 518/520
Florida 165, Buenos Aires
Haroon Chambers, South Napier Road, Karachi
15 Graham Road, Ballard Estate, Bombay 1
17 Central Avenue P.O. Dharamtala, Calcutta
Munsoor Building, Main Street, Colombo 11
Munshi Niketan, near Kamla Market, Ajmeri Gate, Delhi
25 rue Henri Barbusse, Paris 5e
Islands Brygge 5, Copenhagen

FIRST PUBLISHED 1954

SET IN 12PT. BELL TYPE AND PRINTED IN GREAT BRITAIN
BY EBENEZER BAYLIS AND SON, LTD.,
THE TRINITY PRESS, WORCESTER AND LONDON
F.754

THE CONTRIBUTIONS

THE CONTRIBUTIONS

*The frontispiece photograph of Sir Winston Churchill
was taken by Miss Toni Frissell at Blenheim Palace*

To W.S.C.

Lines contributed to this volume by the late Viscount Norwich

When ears were deaf and tongues were mute,
    You told of doom to come.
When others fingered on the flute,
    You thundered on the drum.

When armies marched and cities burned
    And all you said came true,
Those who had mocked your warnings turned
    Almost too late to you.

Then doubt gave way to firm belief,
    And through five cruel years
You gave us glory in our grief,
    And laughter through our tears.

When final honours are bestowed
    And last accounts are done,
Then shall we know how much was owed
    By all the world to one.

Norwich

Prologue

by Professor Gilbert Murray

This book, a serious comment by so many distinguished contemporaries on the great Leader of the Free Nations in the world war, is unique of its kind and ought to be of unique interest to future historians. When I first heard of it, I was reminded of a phrase of Cicero's about Julius Cæsar. The other statesmen of the time, he says, were ordinary human beings; he could reckon more or less what they would say and do: '*Sed hoc* τέρας' — he uses the Greek word τέρας —'But this portent, this prodigy'. . . . About him Cicero's judgment fails him. He cannot be calculated on. How wonderful it would have been, I thought, if there existed some objective contemporary account of that soldier, statesman, scholar, historian, who has so impressed the imagination of the world ever since and whom in his own day so many admired and loved, so many hated, and perhaps no one understood. That is what this book is trying to do for our own τέρας. Of course, a contemporary account can never be quite objective and impersonal; personal feelings are involved; people see things from different angles. But in the case of this book it is clear from the mere list of names that the contributors are not all of one mind; they are not flatterers, they are not partisans.

Cicero attributes to his 'portent': *'incredibilem celeritatem, vigilantiam, industriam'*—unimaginable celerity, vigilance, and industry. We may be reminded of the celerity with which our 'portent' acted at every crisis; the instantaneous response to Russia when Russia became Germany's enemy in the war; the instantaneous offer of union to France when she was stricken down; and the instantaneous appeal to the highest spirit of the nation when we were alone after Dunkirk. And vigilance: who can read the history of the war without astonishment at that eye which kept an apparently unfailing watch on a thousand issues at once, in every corner of the world? Who has not marvelled at the industry which, amid the enormous mass of problems great or small confronting the world-wide interests of British policy, seemed to neglect nothing, to shrink from no decision, to spare itself no labour?

I have little or nothing to add to the record. Of all the writers in this book, I have perhaps the least personal knowledge of the Prime Minister. I have been only a looker-on at politics, though I may claim to have looked on for an unusually long time and with constant interest. I remember without effort the energy, the almost excessive but always generous energy, of Sir Winston Churchill's youth; his military career, his cavalry charges, his escape from imprisonment, his admiration for his Boer enemy; his early political life with its unorthodoxies and adventures. I remember the eager prison reforms, the Dartmoor

Shepherd with his incorrigible taste for sacrilege, the warlike siege of the international gangsters in Sidney Street; and above all, the vigour with which he defended against fierce criticism the splendidly generous Peace of Vereeniging.

I find among my memories various trifles which would be too intimate to mention if I did not reflect how we would treasure such an anecdote if it were recorded of Julius Cæsar. My father-in-law, Lord Carlisle, once happened to call on Miss Stanley—Aunt Maud, as we used to call her—and found her in tears because her ward, Clementine Hozier, had just become engaged to young Mr. Churchill, of whose political ways Aunt Maud did not approve. About a year afterwards the same subject happened to be mentioned, and Aunt Maud said, 'Oh, we all like him so much; he is such a good husband.' If we had such a fact recorded about Cæsar should we not be greatly interested and, I fear, a little surprised?

Another much more recent incident stays in my mind, occurring on a rather curious occasion. A large portrait of Churchill, as First Lord of the Admiralty in the Asquith government, was hanging in the National Liberal Club and received some damage from a bomb. The club had promised, when it was repaired, to present it to him again and show him how it looked; but in the meantime he had become leader of the Conservative Party. He came to receive it and Lord Meston, in the chair, commented on the unusual and perhaps unique situation. Churchill looked round the room with a smile that seemed to be personally addressed to every member of the crowded audience, and said:

'Lord Meston says this is an unusual and almost unique occasion; to me it seems just like old times.' He went on to tell us what I feel is profoundly true, that many Liberal causes, many forms of freedom, of international friendship and simple human happiness, had seemed securely established at the beginning of the century but had one by one been marred or lost or sometimes utterly reversed in the long years of war and mutual suspicion. They must not be forgotten; they must be won again and made safe. That was a task for us and for the whole free world.

And what kind of man does the Free World need as a leader in that task of self-defence and recovery? I will not attempt to say; but as a suggestion or rough sketch of such a leader I am reminded of a character of Churchill which I heard given by another Prime Minister. 'I have often differed from Winston,' he said. 'I have had hard tussles with him, but I will say this for him: he is a hard fighter but he never bears malice; he never intrigues; and he can't tell a lie, because I have seen him try and he turned pink all over.' I do not know if George Washington turned pink when he found that he suffered from the same disability.

Among the distinguished bearers of this present tribute there are members of all political parties. He to whom we pay it has in name changed his party more than once, but in fairness I think he could often plead that he has on the whole maintained the same political attitude while the parties about him have changed theirs. However that may be, there are sometimes crises in history in which the main line of a nation's policy is clear enough to unite the whole nation. At the present time I think that this clear unity of aspiration and interest has occurred not only for our nation but for a whole great unity of nations—for that great whole which we sometimes speak of too vaguely as the Free World, sometimes too narrowly as Western or Christian civilization, meaning that great culture which derives from Jerusalem its monotheism, from Rome its genius for law and government, and from Athens its pursuit of wisdom and beauty and the attainment of a good life for man. However it be defined or described, this civilization is now united in the defence of freedom and the human conscience against new and extraordinary dangers. In that respect it is all Liberal in spirit. It also moves steadily, in varying degrees or speeds, towards relieving by collective social action the inequalities of classes and the disabilities of the poor. It has there its Socialist spirit. Above all, perhaps, at this moment when faced with the open peril of military defeat, or the more subtle perils of gradual economic collapse or even profound unconscious barbarization, it is determined even at great cost to preserve a great and noble civilization from revolution and decay. It is a Conservative spirit. All political watchwords are but half-truths. There is something greater beneath them and above them which commands a more sacred allegiance. To this greater aim I think Churchill has been constantly true. I do not say he has been always right; of no human being can that be said. Of many great world issues we do not yet know the end: but we know on which side he has fought. He has been criticized as too impulsive, too violent; he is certainly free from the weakness, much commoner in political life, of timidity and indecision. He has been described as old-fashioned, as romantic, as aristocratic in his ideals; a charge true, I think, in one sense only, that he has not succumbed to that tendency to subordinate all action to the purely utilitarian or economic motive which is sometimes called 'modern'. He leaves always a place for honour, a place for magnanimity, a place perhaps for that actual love for the traditions and standards of our country and that old Empire which has so often brought to weaker peoples freedom instead of oppression, and peace instead of constant war. It is this feeling which makes him typically patriotic though never for a moment nationalist.

He disclaims in his history of the war any special personal glory. He was only, he says, interpreting the mind of his colleagues; he was certainly, like all democratic leaders, expressing the mind of the country, but he expressed always its nobler mind. An example of this distinction can be seen in his attitude to one crisis which arose after the war, of a kind which in past history has led to terrible results. When supremacy in power has passed from one nation to another the result has often been war, almost always it has been great jealousy and mutual bitterness. It is clear that this country in the war-time was outstripped and as a leader of the world utterly superseded by the United States. We had been the wealthiest of nations; our Fleet had had no equal anywhere; our Empire had maintained the peace of the world. In every point the United States had now surpassed us; most decisive fact of all, it had taken upon its broad shoulders the protection and the restoration of a half-ruined world, while we ourselves were supported upon its bounty. It is a great testimonial to the statesmen of both nations that this supersession has taken place with no breach in our friendship, with nothing worse than a few outbursts of superficial irritation in a few over-sensitive quarters. When the Russian dictator speaks of 'the inevitable war between Great Britain and the United States', which is to come as a result of this crisis, on both sides of the Atlantic that threat is greeted with a smile. Great credit is due to the common sense and good feeling of both nations. But what a lead, what a spontaneous and unhesitating lead has come to the whole movement from Sir Winston Churchill! He typifies in himself that 'mixing up', that intimacy which is more than an alliance, between the great English-speaking communities. He has given towards this blending of patriotisms more than any other Englishman could.

He has also been quicker than others to make clear the general needs of the war-shattered world. At Fulton he emphasized the division between Russia and the Free World at a time when people had not yet recovered from their war-time illusions, and the speech roused wide protests. It took more than a year to be accepted as obvious. Then at Zürich he showed that the answer to that division was closer unity in Europe, and that the first step must be the reconciliation of the old enemies, France and Germany. It seemed an impossible demand, but it is now accepted by the wiser minds in both nations. He said more. He reminded the angry nations that revenge is 'of all indulgences the shortest and the most expensive'. He told them of the one thing that the world needed; 'one simple thing, that some hundreds of millions of men and women should now give their

minds to doing good instead of evil and reaping there-
from blessings instead of curses.' A truism perhaps, a
moralizing commonplace that anyone might say: yes,
but he said it with a voice which made the hundreds of
millions listen and think.

Nearly all war settlements are made in an unwhole-
some atmosphere and are seen to be unsatisfactory soon
after they are made. The last great settlement is no
exception. No one can tell how far the flaws that we
see now were due to Churchill or occurred, as some of
them certainly did, in spite of Churchill, through the
greater influence of other allies, through the accidents
of a complicated struggle, or through the over-master-
ing pressure of facts. Our great European civilization
is left in extreme danger. If we can carry out the
programme of the United Nations and the Zürich
speech, it looks as if we could attain world peace at last
and save civilization. But we have not yet achieved our
unity or completed our organization: we have against
us nations of incalculable power, limitless ambition
and, in our sense of the word, no conscience or fear of
God. We may not succeed in our contest. But if we
follow the lead that Sir Winston Churchill has given
from the day when Britain stood alone in the world war
till the call at Zürich to unite and forgive, we shall at
least be able to feel that we have never yielded to an
enemy, never betrayed a friend, and never failed, so far
as human wisdom could guide us, to strive for the
victory of the right.

Gilbert Murray.

The Churchill Heritage

Genus immortale manet multosque per annos.—VIRGIL

by SIR ARTHUR MACNALTY

THIS book is written as a tribute to a national hero on the occasion of his eightieth birthday. It is a tribute in which the British-speaking peoples can share irrespective of creed, party, or class, for twice in a life-time—although the second achievement in magnitude surpassed the first—has Winston Churchill helped to preserve Great Britain and the British Commonwealth and to save them from enemy domination. It is no exaggerated statement to add that all the free peoples of the world share in this debt of gratitude and are not unmindful of their liberation from tyranny and servitude. It was because Winston Churchill led Great Britain when she stood alone in the struggle against Hitler that cataclysmic disaster did not occur, and that freedom was preserved for the whole world.

Others in this book will speak of these achievements with fuller knowledge and greater authority. It is this writer's privilege to act as opening chorus and like ancient Gower 'to sing a song that old was sung'; to recall to mind Winston Churchill's heritage, the great examples of his ancestors, which encouraged him from his earliest youth to emulate and at length to surpass them.[1]

Service to King, Queen, and Country is traditional in the Churchill family. It is an ancient stock of the west country. Some genealogists trace it back to the Norman Conquest and beyond it. Churchill in Somerset is the name-place of the family. Omitting the chronicle of several warrior Churchills, in the seventeenth century we come to John Churchill, barrister-at-law of the Middle Temple, and a Deputy Registrar of the Court of Chancery, and his wife, Sarah, the daughter and co-heiress of Sir Henry Winstone of Standish in Gloucestershire. Their son was Winston Churchill, who was born at Wootton Glanville in Dorset in 1620.

Winston Churchill, the first, like his illustrious descendant and namesake, was a man of remarkable abilities. A scholar, he left Oxford to serve in the Royalist army, fought in several battles and was severely wounded, and with his wife, Elizabeth, in 1646 sought a refuge from the oppression of the Commonwealth under his mother-in-law's roof at Ashe House, near Axminster, for Lady Drake was a resolute Puritan. The Winston Churchills had twelve children of whom seven died in infancy. Winston has been regarded as one of the most notable and potent of sires. His daughter, Arabella, had a son by King James II. This was the Duke of Berwick, one of Louis XIV's famous generals, who won the Battle of Almanaza; his third son, John,

[1] Acknowledgment is made to Essential Books Limited for permission to reprint in this chapter certain passages from the Author's book, *The Three Churchills*.

born in 1650, was the future Duke of Marlborough, the great captain of his age; his second surviving son, George, became an admiral and head of the Admiralty; his third surviving son, Charles, was a distinguished general. It is not therefore surprising to find Galton quoting the Churchill family as one of his chief examples of hereditary genius.

John Churchill's childhood was spent at Ashe House, where his strict upbringing taught him to be prudent and economical and to check the expression of his feelings. It also inspired him with ambition and fixity of purpose.

With the coming of King Charles II, Winston's services were rewarded by restoration of his estate at Mintern, a knighthood, and office. He became Member of Parliament for Weymouth, and was elected one of the early Fellows of the Royal Society; his namesake inspected his signature in the Roll of Fellows on receiving the same high distinction. Now Sir Winston did what he could for his sons.

After a year at the City Free School, Dublin, and two years at St. Paul's School, London, John Churchill at the age of fifteen was given a pair of colours by the Duke of York, who noted his enthusiasm and promise. The boy received his baptism of fire at the siege of Tangier against the Moors, and later was in the Duke of York's flagship at the indecisive naval battle of Sole Bay against the Dutch. When fighting for France as a volunteer under the leadership of Marshal Turenne, he not only learned the French art of making war, but also became familiar with French strategy, tactics, and psychological approach to problems of warfare. He was commended for his conspicuous bravery by Louis XIV and Turenne, and Charles II made him a lieutenant-colonel.

Now he met the one and abiding love of his life. He married in 1678 Miss Sarah Jennings, maid of honour to the Duchess of York, and both he and his wife advanced in court favour. The accession of his patron, James II, made him Baron Churchill. John Churchill, opposed to James's Roman Catholic policy, joined William of Orange when the Protestant wind wafted that monarch to England, and became Earl of Marlborough and a privy councillor.

So far, Churchill's career had been one of triumphal progress, but in 1692 he was arrested and sent to the Tower on a charge of high treason. The evidence was proved to be fabricated and Churchill was released to live in retirement. In 1699, he was restored to favour by King William, and on that monarch's death and the accession of Queen Anne, he was appointed at the age of fifty-two Captain General of the Queen's Forces, Master of Ordnance, and created Knight of the Garter. After this, as Professor Smyth of Cambridge said, 'To write the life of Marlborough is to write the history of the reign of Queen Anne.' In her reign he achieved imperishable fame as soldier, statesman, and diplomatist.

'More, perhaps, than any other man,' observed Sir Archibald Alison, 'Marlborough was the architect of England's greatness; for he at once established on a solid basis the Protestant succession, which secured its religious freedom, and vanquished the formidable enemy which threatened its national independence.' He is not only the greatest general that this country has ever produced, but one of the greatest generals of all time.

He fought ten campaigns in the course of which he never lost a battle or failed to take a town or fortress to which he laid siege. As with Turenne, age never diminished his boldness and imagination. Few generals of his years would have dared to make that brilliant march into the heart of Germany leaving an undefeated French army in Flanders, and have staked the fortunes of the Grand Alliance on the Battle of Blenheim. He assumed heavy burdens and in spite of them accomplished much. He was constantly opposed and thwarted in his strategy by the Dutch deputies, his own officers, the German princes, and the imperialists. He met with ingratitude. He was betrayed by Harley and Bolingbroke, who owed their place to his good offices, and deserted by his Queen, whom he ever served with loyal devotion. He bore prosperity and misfortune with equal courage and patience. While he was bold and adventurous in war, he was never rash. His plans were so carefully matured and prepared beforehand, that it was said his battles were almost won before they were fought. Everything was overseen by himself—the provisioning, footwear, and clothing for the troops, the hospitals, and arrangements for the care of the sick and wounded on the field, including those of the defeated enemy. He was beloved by his soldiers, who called him 'Our Corporal'.

His courage at all times was superb. He repeatedly led his troops into action, had horses killed under him, exposed himself fearlessly under heavy fire, in spite of the entreaties of the Queen, the Government, his officers, and his wife, and always emerged unscathed. His mental and physical energy and industry were remarkable. He often suffered from headaches, probably attacks of migraine, yet after a busy day spent in inspections, councils of war, and interviews with dignitaries and members of his staff, he would sit down and write letters and dispatches by the light of a solitary candle. In those midnight hours on active service, he governed England for his Queen and swayed the policy of Europe.

For ten years Marlborough had the general direction of the war in Flanders and Spain. At the same time he watched political movements at home and conducted negotiations with the allies of England. His duties as commander-in-chief were exacting, yet unceasing demands were made on his energies and time in the interests of his country. In an age when communications were imperfect and travelling arduous, he crossed the Channel to persuade Queen Anne to change one of her Ministers, or sped to Altranstädt to prevent Charles XII bringing his veteran Swedish army to the aid of France. His diplomacy kept the Margrave of Baden and the Elector of Hanover in the Alliance, and more than once he hurried to Berlin to conciliate the offended King of Prussia. He reconciled the Emperor with his insurgent Hungarian subjects, aided the Calvinists of the Cevennes in revolt, provided aid to the Duke of Savoy, and improved British relations with Portugal.

These great qualities were joined to serenity, courtesy, and a natural dignity which were never ruffled either in council or on the battlefield by fatigue, haste, agitation, or ill-temper. Above all, he was endowed with the gift of patience. He wrote and proved in his career that 'Patience will overcome all things,' and again, 'As I think most things are governed by destiny, having done

all things we should submit with patience.' Devotion to
his God and the Church of England and service to his
Queen and country guided his life.

In a dissolute age he was a pattern of domesticity,
true and faithful to his wayward Sarah. He wrote her
wonderful love letters in all his campaigns. 'Pray believe me,' he would often add, 'when I assure you that
I love you more than I can express.' After the accession
of George I, Marlborough passed the remaining years
of his life in retirement. His mental and physical powers
gradually decayed, and on 16 June 1722, the end came.
Sarah survived her husband by twenty-two years, dying
at the age of eighty-four in 1744.

Marlborough had many contemporary enemies. Their
slanders and the erroneous judgment of Macaulay and
Thackeray clouded the reputation of one of Great
Britain's greatest benefactors. There is no need here to
recall the charges of double dealing, of undue prolonga-
tion of the war, of peculation and of avarice which have
been made against John Churchill. These have been
more or less refuted by impartial biographers and completely by his descendant, Winston Churchill, in the
authoritative biography written with full access to the
Blenheim papers and with many new sources of information. This has been termed one of the three or four finest
works of historical scholarship to appear in its decade.
Mr. A. L. Rowse in a lecture at the Royal Institution,
delivered in 1944, on 'Mr. Churchill and English History', has sketched the close resemblance between the
careers of the two Churchills. 'Each had been the dip-
lomatic and political brain-centre of a grand alliance
against a great aggressor.' It is rare for the man of

action to be also the thinker and historian. Winston Churchill, the soldier, only laid down the sword to take up the pen. Winston Churchill, the statesman, only left office to write the life of Marlborough. Lord Balfour and Lord Rosebery had both suggested it to him as an hereditary duty, and he had long meditated this great task before entering upon it.

Henrietta, the wife of Francis, Earl of Godolphin, became Duchess of Marlborough on her father's death. She died in 1733 and was succeeded by her nephew, Charles, the second son of Anne Churchill and the third Earl of Sunderland, as third Duke. At the Battle of Dettingen, 1743, he commanded a brigade and fought with all John Churchill's courage. He raised a force for King George II in the Jacobite rising of 1745. In 1758 he led a raid on St. Malo against the French. Later in the year he commanded a contingent of ten thousand English troops sent to join Prince Ferdinand's campaign in Western Germany, but died of dysentery at Munster. He was a Knight of the Garter and a Fellow of the Royal Society. His son, George, was Lord Chancellor of the Household, 1762–3, and Lord Privy Seal, 1763–5. The seventh Duke, John Winston Spencer Churchill, 'a sensible, honourable, and industrious public man', was born in 1822 and succeeded to the title in 1857. From 1876 to 1880 he was Lord Lieutenant of Ireland in Lord Beaconsfield's government. His administration was popular and he did his best to promote Irish welfare and industries. When he died in 1883, the mantle of statesmanship fell on his third son, Lord Randolph Churchill.

As John Churchill achieved his highest fame in the reign of Queen Anne, so Lord Randolph Churchill's

[16]

whole life and meteoric career passed in the long and successful reign of Queen Victoria. Among her statesmen he will always be remembered for the services he rendered to his country and for the high promise which a cruel destiny prevented him from fulfilling. His deeds are the theme of two important works. Winston Churchill's *Life of Lord Randolph Churchill*, in which filial affection is blended with sound political appraisement, reveals Lord Randolph's fine qualities and ranks as one of the chief political biographies. Lord Rosebery's study is an admirable tribute. Its prose has often been cited as a model of perfect English.

Lord Randolph Churchill was born in London on 13 February 1849. Educated at Eton and Merton College, Oxford, at the University he took an honours degree in the school of law and modern history in 1870. In 1874 he entered Parliament as a Conservative and married a beautiful American, Miss Jeanette Jerome, whose wit equalled her charm. It was a year of happiness and success.

While his father was Lord Lieutenant of Ireland, Lord Randolph studied Irish affairs so thoroughly that he was able subsequently to speak of them with authority and understanding. As a 'free lance', he led the 'Fourth Party' in the House of Commons, which not only assailed Mr. Gladstone and his government with scorn and invective, but inveighed against the 'masterly inactivity' of the Conservative policy. His personal charm and gifts of oratory were used to advocate his belief in Tory democracy and his fervent desire to promote social reform. 'Trust the people and they will trust you,' he said at Belfast in 1884 to an enthusiastic audience. By his talents and forcefulness he organized the Conservatives, destroyed the party caucus, and was officially accepted as one of the Conservative leaders.

In November 1884, with some foreknowledge of his future labours, he went to India where he visited the chief cities, studied the political situation, and discussed self-government with a number of Indian reformers. On this question he was ahead of his day and generation. Soon after his return to England, the Opposition defeated Mr. Gladstone's government with the temporary support of the Irish Nationalists. Lord Salisbury's first government only lasted from June 1885 to February 1886; in it Lord Randolph Churchill was appointed Secretary of State for India.

In office, Lord Randolph showed himself a capable administrator. He settled a critical negotiation with Russia over the Afghan frontier, strengthened the defences of India, put down King Theebaw's savage misrule in Burma, and annexed that country to the British Empire. His Indian budget evoked the admiration of the House of Commons. His speech on it was eloquent and gave a wide survey of Indian affairs. The fall of the Government prevented Churchill from bringing in other measures including a comprehensive inquiry into Indian affairs. Nevertheless, he had achieved remarkable results within a short time.

Mr. Gladstone now became Prime Minister, supported by the Irish Nationalists. He introduced his Home Rule Bill for Ireland in April in the midst of a political agitation against it in which Lord Randolph was the foremost leader. The Prime Minister split the Liberal Party by his action, and at the ensuing General Election the

Unionists gained a large majority. Lord Salisbury formed a Conservative government in which Lord Randolph Churchill became Chancellor of the Exchequer and leader of the House of Commons at the early age of thirty-seven. It was a rise to high office comparable with that of the younger Pitt, as Sir Winston Churchill observes.

Lord Randolph now considered the time had come to transmute his democratic ideas and beliefs into practice for the good of his country. In this faith he was again ahead of his time. Had he been more prudent, he would have waited to convince his colleagues of the necessity for these reforms. But he had some justification for thinking that he could carry the Conservative Party with him in this policy. He was popular and had a great following in the country. Moreover, the Cabinet had approved his famous Dartford speech which outlined a broad programme of social reform.

The culminating crisis arose when Churchill brought his budget proposals before the Cabinet. It was a brilliant budget and an economical one. It would have replanned the national revenue, reduced existing taxes, devised new taxes, adjusted taxation according to means, transferred taxes from necessities to luxuries, provided money for a new system of local government, and made economies in the Service departments and the national expenditure generally. The Cabinet received it with dismay. Lord Salisbury supported the opposers of this budget and Lord Randolph resigned. The real issue was no mere wrangle over Army estimates, but a profound disagreement between the Chancellor and his Cabinet colleagues on the subject of Tory democracy;

and the resignation came not from pique and arrogance but on a question of high principle.

Hitherto, Lord Randolph had been impatient. In the ensuing years he showed all the patience of his great ancestor, Marlborough. He might have split the Conservatives by leading a new party to champion the cause of Tory democracy; alternatively, he might have joined the Liberals. Either course was repugnant to him. The years went by, he served on committees, won the Oaks in 1889, visited Russia and South Africa, and waited patiently for the tide to turn and to be given opportunity once more to exercise his great gifts in the government of his country. In 1892 there was a false dawn. He was reconciled with the Conservatives, invited to sit on the front Opposition bench, recognized again as one of the party leaders, and delivered a speech against the second Home Rule Bill full of wise statesmanship. High office in the next Conservative government was prophesied for him. This was not to be; a severe illness intervened and he died on 24 January, 1895.

Yet in retrospect his career was not a failure. Much of what he strove for has been effected, and far-reaching health and social reforms have come in the course of years. For these he pledged his faith and his career.

In his elder son, Winston Churchill, Lord Randolph Churchill left behind him a great gift to the British people, the son who, in his own eloquent words, 'was to lift again the flag he found lying on a stricken field'.

Such is the Churchill heritage, such were the men who made it. Endowed with such an heritage, Winston

Churchill's soul was kindled with desire to follow his ancestors' shining example of service to the British people. In the gravest hour of national peril it was given to him to bring the nation out of the dark valleys to the heights of freedom.

Arthur S. MacNalty

The Man of Peace

by Viscount Cecil

THE purpose of this book is to commemorate what we all owe to those who led our country through the period of the two World Wars and especially to Sir Winston Churchill. Of his technical military capacity I have nothing to say that would be worth anyone's while to read. But there are certain aspects of himself on which, as a contemporary, I might have something to say.

One thing there is that impresses me very much. It is the unity of his personality. From the time he left Harrow to the present day he has had a passion for combat. Resistance to evil is a general human feeling and in some natures it easily combines with patriotism to become a passion. The impulse to throw one's whole self into the righteous defence of that which a man values for his friends, his family, and his country is with some men strong and if it involves personal danger it may become absorbing.

That is a common feeling, as it has always been. Nor has it been destroyed by the change from monarchy to democracy in so many European countries. In our own, the rise of a Commonwealth of independent States, united under one Sovereign, has perhaps increased it. In its lesser form of nationalism it is almost universal. And certainly it has been a powerful influence with Sir Winston. But there is another element in his character. As he said early in his public life, all he cared for was the defeat of the Germans. When, in 1918, he visited the British front with Clemenceau, he was asked to remonstrate with the old statesman for spending too much time under fire. He did so, but accepted and agreed with the characteristic excuse: '*C'est mon grand plaisir.*' Danger is no doubt attractive in itself to men like this just as crossing the Pacific on a raft or climbing the peaks of Mount Everest are fascinating to other similar spirits. So it is that from the time he left Harrow to the present day, active service in war has been to him the most absorbing of all pursuits. Indeed, it may be said to have dominated his life. His early reading was directly or indirectly on military subjects. When he was twenty he joined the Army and for the next years he went either as an officer or as a military correspondent to Cuba, to India, to South Africa—wherever he could see and take part in military operations.

He entered Parliament when he was twenty-six and joined in the ordinary political life of the House of Commons. But looking back on it, one can see that what really interested him was the idea of combat and the necessity of adequate preparation for it.

It was the struggle, combined, no doubt, with the danger to himself, which was the attraction. For war as an institution, as a means of settling international

c

disputes, he had a horror, as he explained in one of his earlier Parliamentary speeches when he talked of 'breaking hearts and straitened means' as an inevitable result of European war. That was why he became such a convinced and vehement supporter of the League of Nations. As early as 1932 he refers to the League as 'a priceless instrument of peace'.[1] So at about the same time he declares: 'We should adhere to the League.' Even though it may not be sufficiently influential in 'far off Asia', still, it should be of the greatest help in 'recreating a Concert of Europe, in restraining the war-like propensities of the German nation' and in 're-dressing her grievances'.[2] So in 1934 he thinks that the League should be the great instrument upon which peace should centre. He urges all Powers to lay their anxieties before the League and hopes that regional agreements under the sanction and authority of the League will be formed to repress aggression, an idea to which he has recently returned. So he believes in 1935 that our one great hope for peace is in 'a system of collective security under the League'[3] and in a very eloquent passage urges perseverance in this policy. It is with no surprise, therefore, that we find how deeply he deplored the failure of this country to utilize the League in the protection of Abyssinia against Italy.

Again, in his speeches before the outbreak of the Second World War he returns to the subject. Thus in 1936 he says: 'Horrible war, blasting in its devastation the prosperity of the world, can only be prevented by the marshalling of preponderant forces, sustained by

[1] See *Arms and the Covenant.*
[2] ibid.
[3] ibid.

world opinion, as a deterrent to any aggressor who breaks the Peace'; and again in 1937 he calls for trust in the moral forces enshrined in the League of Nations, pledged to resist the action of the aggressor.

It will be observed from these quotations—and they could be multiplied—that Sir Winston was no pacifist. On the contrary, he was convinced that force should be just as available to suppress international crime as it is in all civilized countries to control individual criminals.

This is what made him ready at all times to throw himself with all his knowledge and energies into the fight to preserve freedom and justice as the basis of peace. To him it was, and always has been, the supreme duty of a patriotic citizen. It is tempting to believe that he foresaw such a call as came to him in the Second World War and prepared himself for it. Certainly such a prevision would explain his whole life from his school days to the present time. I have heard him compared with other great men in our history, notably Lord Chatham. But there is none of them who had this unity of purpose. It is as if a fairy godmother had from his birth warned him that he would spend his life in struggling, alas, in vain, to preserve peace. And he prepared himself accordingly, so that, in response to a summons by his King and Country, he was able to organize and inspire the wonderful effort by which the aggressor was driven back in defeat.

In the fifth volume of his history of the war, *Closing the Ring*, there is a passage which vividly illustrates what I am trying to say. I refer to the meeting in 1943 at Teheran of Churchill, Roosevelt, and Stalin, with their Staffs. A Conference had taken place there at which the invasion of Occupied France from the sea had been decided upon and a final dinner was held of a social character. Someone asked what should be done to the Germans after the war. Stalin replied by saying that there were only about 50,000 Germans who were real militarists and they should be killed. Here was the policy of ruthless destruction for its own sake. Instantly came Churchill's rejection. 'I would rather be shot myself than agree to such a plan.' And when someone, half seriously, seemed to support the Russian proposal, he rose and left the room. Stalin and Vyshinsky, alarmed at so serious a danger to the Alliance, hurried after him and assured him that he was taking the proposal too seriously. He was pacified, but the incident shows that the man who was ready for every effort and every sacrifice to secure the triumph in battle of the great principles for which he fought would have nothing to do with mere barbaric slaughter.

This, then, seems to me one great lesson of Churchill's life. He is, no doubt, as others have explained, a man of great ability, industry, eloquence, and courage. In these qualities he has had predecessors in our country; great rulers like some of our sovereigns; great statesmen like the younger Pitt, who wore himself out in defence of his country; great soldiers who, like Wellington, regarded victory as a tragedy only less terrible than defeat. But there have been none who have, like Churchill, combined a loathing of war with playing a chief part in defeating an enemy as determined and powerful as any by which we have been assailed in our history.

His early training belonged to the period of the

Balance of Power, secured by military alliances. It was, indeed, the road by which he reached his advocacy of an international organization for Peace. That the chief of British international interests was the maintenance of peace was an ancient maxim of British foreign policy, dating from the time when we abandoned the idea of having a European continental Empire. It was, I suppose, emphasized by the surrender of Calais and the defeat of the Spanish Armada. From that time forward, no British statesman ever advocated a policy of aggression in Europe. We took part, indeed, in European controversy and even in European war. We fought the French repeatedly, and later on the Germans and the Russians. But our object was in all cases defensive—to ward off the danger of invasion. We were determined to resist invasion and, indeed, to take whatever steps were required to prevent any of our continental neighbours from embarking on such a policy. From this position it was a natural step to support an organization the object of which was to secure peace by the international prevention of military aggression. That is, indeed, the only alternative to the old policy of a Balance of Power resting on a system of alliances.

It is—and should be—one of the chief reasons for our admiration and support of Sir Winston Churchill that he has consistently advocated peace by international understanding. No doubt there must be adequate preparation for military resistance to foreign aggression in the last resort. But that should be consistent with an organization for the peaceable discussion and, if possible, the settlement of all disputes likely to lead to war. That, indeed, is fundamental to all civilized Government—national or international. The overwhelming opinion of mankind desires peace, based on justice, and many of us believe that this result is most likely to be secured by a formal appeal to public opinion, secured by open and impartial discussion. If that fails, resort to force is all that remains. But surely Sir Winston is right in regarding modern war, with all the additional horrors which human ingenuity has invented, as a terrible alternative. It is a striking confirmation of what is here written that Sir Winston Churchill should have stated as lately as 10 October 1953, that he continues to bear the burden of office because he feels that he may have an influence on what he cares about above all else—'the building of a sure and lasting peace.'

Cecil

Churchill's Use of English Speech

by THE LATE VISCOUNT SIMON

SIR WINSTON CHURCHILL has told us how greatly in his early days he admired the writings of Gibbon and of Macaulay. These two authors were well read in the classics and it may be the study of them had something to do with the appreciation of classical form that has always characterized the Prime Minister's literary judgments. For, in spite of Harrow, he owes nothing to the classics at first hand. There are passages in his *Marlborough* which almost remind one of the language of that Roman historian who wrote: 'When they make a Wilderness, they call it Peace', or the still more famous judgment: 'By consent of all he was well qualified to rule—if he had not ruled.' But Sir Winston, while writing or speaking with the rotundity of a truly classical style, is not only sardonic, like the author of the *Decline and Fall*, or antithetical, like him and Macaulay, and there is more cheerful humour than ironic point in his words: neither Gibbon nor Macaulay would have made us laugh with 'ter-minological inexactitude'—or with 'some chicken—some neck'.

The best English combines the use of short sentences with sentences that are long drawn out with Glad-stonian exuberance. It sometimes employs mono-syllables and then makes use of a vocabulary of longer words. Who can say whether it is better to have written 'After life's fitful fever, he sleeps well' (which Matthew Arnold held to be the touchstone of real poetry), or to have used a phrase like 'the multitudinous seas incarnadine'? Should one prefer the simple words, 'the paths of glory lead but to the grave', which ring in the mind like a passing-bell, or Gray's lines in the same poem about 'a gem of purest ray serene' that 'the dark unfathomed caves of ocean bear'? Churchill shows by the language which he uses, as do many of our best writers and orators, how truly he appreciates this double excellence of the English tongue in the mouth of a man who knows how to use it.

I doubt if this double virtue is to be found in some other tongues. Save for Gretchen's song at her spin-ning-wheel in *Faust*, German seems to be a 'sesquipe-dalian' language, and to an English ear the long words in French classical poetry sound a weak equivalent of the Latin nouns from which they are derived.

The man who said, when he became Prime Minister, 'I have nothing to offer but blood, toil, tears, and sweat' knew well the full effect of a succession of monosyllables. Stanley Baldwin knew it too, for Baldwin once said:[1]

[1] In the House of Commons, 16th February, 1923.

The English language is the richest in the world in monosyllables. Four words, of one syllable each . . . contain salvation for this country and the whole world, and they are Faith, Hope, Love, and Work. No Government in this country to-day which has not faith in the people, hope in the future, love for its fellow-men, and which will not work and work, and work, will ever bring this country through into better days and better times, or will ever bring Europe through or the world through.

There is also a remarkable example of the use of such words in the poem of Tennyson, which Mr. Menzies once quoted with reference to the new situation of the British Commonwealth:

Tho' much is taken much abides; and tho'
We are not now that strength which in old days
Moved earth and heaven; that which we are, we are;
One equal temper of heroic hearts,
Made weak by time and fate, but strong in will
To strive, to seek, to find, and not to yield.

Fifty monosyllables in fifty-six words!

One of the reasons for Churchill's addiction to monosyllabic speech is his dislike of the use of unnecessary adjectives. He wants on occasion to cut down the expression of his thought to the bare bones and only uses an epithet when it adds something. Anyone who has been his colleague in settling the terms of a King's Speech knows his fastidious judgment in these respects. Adjectives in an English sentence are to many people mere padding, but with Churchill an adjective is used as a sort of supercharger to add to the explosive force of the noun it qualifies. Not for him are those all but meaningless epithets which Lewis Carroll represented as being recommended to the would-be poet, with the result that his protégé produced the lines:

> The wild man went his weary way
> To the strange and lonely pump—

lines for which the young aspirant was reproved, with the warning:

> Such epithets, like pepper, add zest to what you
> write,
> But if you lay them on too thick, you spoil the
> matter quite.

Churchill's skill in the use of words has another quality which his countrymen gratefully recognize. Throughout the war he put into memorable phrases the sentiments which many of us felt but few could express.

He has a real reverence for English speech and uses it with the same loving care with which a violinist, who knows the content and cadences of fine music, plays his own compositions upon the fiddle. Turgenev, the Russian novelist, has somewhere recorded his own sensations when he uses his native tongue. He wrote:

In days of doubt, in days of heavy reflection on the fortunes of my homeland, thou alone art my support and prop, O great, mighty, true and free Russian language. It is impossible to believe that such a language was not given to a great nation.

Churchill, with his memory stored with quotations, feels the same.

So, among his many gifts of utterance, who does not realize that Sir Winston has the power of using English speech not only to rouse his countrymen to fresh effort and to concentrate their resolve, but to establish our mother-tongue as the finest means of human communication in the world?

Simon

The Politician

by Colin Coote

It is difficult to say why the term 'politician' should have acquired a slightly denigratory and derisory connotation. Of those who have made public affairs their career in my lifetime, practically all have been respectable; quite a few have been able; and one or two have even been right. Yet when one calls so and so a 'politician', one generally implies that he or she is more or less contemptible. If one wants to say that so and so is not so bad after all, one calls him or her a statesman—or possibly a stateswoman.

When therefore I accept the invitation to write about Sir Winston Churchill as a politician, I wish to make it clear that the application of the description to him implies no sort of disrespect. Indeed, if the term means a person adept at the art of ingratiating himself with his fellow-countrymen, Sir Winston must be set down as a poor politician. As he has said himself, 'I have a tendency, against which I should, perhaps, be on my guard, to swim against the stream.' Judged by the test of successfully achieving popularity, Churchill has been greatly inferior to many lesser men. The explanation may perhaps be found in the remark made to me by a Frenchman at a time which discretion compels me to conceal that the British had once been ruled by men of character and now had to put up with men of brains. Churchill has never been clever enough to conceal his cleverness, which is quite indispensable if you want to keep the affections of the majority of the British people. He never had a secure electoral base until, quite recently, Woodford acquired that honour. No part of the country smaller than the whole country is Churchill's country. No sectional interest has ever been his special interest. He never commanded the unquestioning party adulation granted to Mr. Whatshisname or Mr. Never Mind. Though never disinclined to take office, a refusal to compromise in order to get it kept him out of it for eleven years; and if it be objected that he has often changed his party, I would be prepared to argue that the changes have been made only to suit unchanging views.

I must try to analyse what, in this country, we mean by 'politician' when we are not hurling it in an injurious fashion at our opponents. We mean essentially what the term means etymologically, namely, one who occupies himself with the arts of advocating or assailing, initiating or defeating, applying or reversing measures concerned with the affairs of the realm. More simply, a politician is one who can get himself elected, and explain and defend himself in the House of Commons after election. Churchill is not so good in the first part of this job; but he is superb in the second. 'I am a child of the House of Commons,' he has truly said. Westminster is his ambience—his aura, as a spiritualist would say. His style of oratory and of repartee, his profound sense of history, his sensitivity to atmosphere —all make him better in Parliament than on the platform. It is only a whimsy, but I have sometimes fancied that when he speaks the packed benches of the House of Commons become an impersonal blur from which the ghosts of Fox, Burke, Addison, Pitt, Macaulay emerge to replace Smith, Jones, Robinson, Atkins, and Snooks.

Even in my lifetime the fashion of Parliamentary oratory has changed. When I first heard it there were still echoes of that rotundity of phrasing and literary tang which pervaded and graced the speeches of the late nineteenth-century giants. A reference to the classics was not considered snobbish and slightly indelicate, and a display of emotion caused no lifting of eyebrows. Between the wars, the fashion changed. Statistics became all the rage, and the production of figures showing the number of red-headed married men in the mining industry was considered irrefutable proof of profundity of knowledge and of thought. A completely matter-of-fact conversational style became the common and most popular form in debate. To-day —thanks probably to the sharper divisions between the main parties—there seems to be some return to the style of dialectical cut and thrust. It must be said, however, that, through all the variations of style, success in Parliament has continued to depend on knowing your stuff. Woe to the man who makes a speech on some recondite topic in the hope that his audience knows nothing about it and will be impressed. Somebody will emerge on the back-benches who has made that topic his life study.

The secret of Sir Winston's success in debate is not his frills but his substance. He knows what he is talking about; and, like Cromwell's captain, so obviously 'loves what he knows'. It is hard to believe, but nevertheless true, that he had no other natural aptitude for oratory at all. The person whose entrance paper to Harrow was a blank sheet of paper cannot be accused of possessing those inegalitarian academic qualifications which Socialists so hotly and queerly resent—even in their own intellectuals. The young man who read nothing until he was a cavalry subaltern in Bangalore may serve as a useful advertisement for the educational system of Mme. Montessori, but was not naturally equipped when he entered the House of Commons to swap *obiter dicta* with Augustine Birrell or to analyse the philosophy of doubt as expounded by Mr. A. J. Balfour. But he had imbibed the sonorous cadences of Gibbon. He had an instinct for the English tongue, even though Latin was mysterious gibberish. Moreover, we are, I believe, biologically speaking, exactly half our father and half our mother; and on both sides his natural endowments were immense. A father who—as fathers found it quite natural to do in those days—rarely cast him a look or a word, transmitted to him a retentive and almost rapacious memory (in spite of 'forgetting Goschen'), and inspired him with the desire of political emulation and vindication. His mother 'shone for him like the evening star'—and his phrases shone like it too, however much they owed, at the outset, to the midnight oil.

[37]

It is perhaps from Lord Randolph Churchill of the Fourth Party that he derives his acute sense of parliamentary tactics. There are two ways of getting on in the House of Commons—by being very naughty, and by being very good. If you are very naughty, your party says, 'Give the puppy a nice bone to keep him quiet'; or, alternatively, your opponents say, 'This is a very able young hound, whom we should like to bark for us.' If you are very good, your party says, 'Ah, here is a well-behaved, house-trained, reliable puppy. Let's give him a nice basket.' You can progress either by being a nuisance, or by being a nonentity. Winston Churchill was never capable of being a nonentity; but he was a most infernal nuisance.

A remarkable feature of the House of Commons is the persistence of belief in the virtues of debate, even when it is known that what is said will not have the slightest effect on what is done. The belief is not, however, ill-founded. What is said is addressed to a wider audience (or was when the Press had the space to report it) and debate is rather like a Rugger trial. It does not much matter whether the Whites or the Colours win, but some players may show themselves capable of scoring tries for England.

It is, of course, much easier to make a successful speech in agreement with the views of the majority. But many of Sir Winston's speeches have been made against the prevailing views of the House and of his own side; and a really hostile House of Commons is like his description of the Wahabis—'austere, intolerant, well-armed and bloodthirsty.' That is why I think his greatest Parliamentary performance (whether you agree with the argument or not) was his defence of the action taken against General Dyer, who had ordered his troops to open fire on the mob in Amritsar in 1921. Edwin Montagu, the Secretary of State for India, had, as he said to me, sat on this egg until it was addled, with the result that he provoked the House to frenzy with a diatribe against 'Prussianism'. On the angriest House I have ever seen, Churchill inflicted a thirty-minute disquisition on military law. It was as dull as a poultice, and as a poultice it drew out the inflammation. Then, to an audience bored into quiescence, he gently administered the Government's case. The Munich speech was brave, but it rebounded from an impermeable carapace of wishful thinking. The wartime speeches were national lyrics, but they expressed the mood and temper of the nation—they answered a want; they did not change a trend.

There are, of course, other tests of parliamentary quality besides speeches. One of the most searching is replies to supplementary questions. Question Time, when Ministers are exposed to back-bench bombardment, is one of the few weapons left to the legislature against the executive; and the ordeal most dreaded by those who are not quick in the uptake. The Irish were first class at getting barbed wit into their questions. One instance, which occurs to me, is Tim Healy's supplementary, after the Secretary for War had answered a question about how many mules and horses had been sent to South Africa during the Boer War. 'Can the Rt. Hon. Gentleman say how many asses have been sent to South Africa?'

It has become extremely dangerous to try the supplementary on Sir Winston Churchill. His replies are like vintage port—they have improved as he has aged. The 'terminological inexactitude' of nearly half a century ago is, of course, famous; but it was part of a prepared answer. The spontaneous quips of later years are legion. 'The Honourable Gentleman should not generate more indignation than he can conveniently contain.' 'I do not need prodding. In fact, if anything, I am a prod.' 'My views are a harmonious process, which keeps them in relation to the current movements of events.' These are samples of vintages from 1927 to 1952. But their bouquet cannot really be appreciated without witnessing Sir Winston's technique at Question Time—the sighting of the victim—the twinkle—the pounce—the manifest enjoyment (sometimes shared with the victim himself). People's public performances in Parliament, whether in debate or at Question Time are the most obvious criteria of their calibre; but not the only criteria. Parliamentary competence is a matter of much more than chat and back-chat. The famous British illogicality is such that we are convinced that our parliamentary institutions are the finest in the world; and, too often, simultaneously contend that M.P.s, who work the institutions, are a lot of overpaid moronic gabblers, mouthing witticisms in the smoking-room and strawberries on the terrace. In fact, the social and nutritional amenities at Westminster are extremely meagre; and the saying that the House of Commons is 'the best club in London' has become a poor joke.

There is, of course, a corporate life, participation in which is part of the job of a good parliamentarian. There is a deep-rooted sympathy between all those who are genuinely devoted to parliamentary institutions; and this sympathy is a prominent characteristic of Sir Winston Churchill. He has never confined his affections to those on his own side of the House. It is equally true that he has always been liked by some members in all parties, and never by all members of one party. He does not seek to keep his side together by any back-slapping effusiveness. Nor, on the other hand, is there anything of the acid aloofness of a Parnell about him. He has a circle of oldest and closest friends—not necessarily all bosom friends of each other; and to them he shows an undeviating loyalty. But he has never shown the slightest inclination for the political coulisses at Westminster. That side of parliamentarianism is not his side.

Nor is he among those who base their parliamentary eminence upon detailed knowledge of procedure. Such a knowledge is no inconsiderable weapon in the parliamentary arsenal—it was, for example, one of the late James Maxton's claims to respect. Most people, however, and Churchill among them, pick up enough knowledge of procedure as they go along to get along; and a lack of a textual knowledge of Erskine May does not make them any the worse parliamentarians. A sea-lawyer is not necessarily the best sailor.

It follows from what I have said of the House of Commons' respect for expertise that a good parliamentarian must also be a good administrator—otherwise he cannot either respond for a Department when a Minister or criticize a Department as a back-bencher. You can learn how to make a speech—you can even read one, though the House likes an appearance of impromptu and does not like too obvious an adherence to a written brief. (In Churchill's case, nobody would have suspected, if he had not confessed it, that in his early days he was incapable of stringing two sentences together without preparation; and memorized in advance his every utterance.)

But what you cannot do, without hard work, is to explain or to attack a Bill. There are, it is true, under the gallery always a bevy of Civil Service Aarons ready to uphold the hands of a Ministerial Moses. There is also an unofficial prompter in the shape of a Parliamentary Private Secretary, on the bench behind you. But, in my experience, in politics thought transference is a broken reed. However well you know the subject, you cannot satisfactorily transmit your knowledge to somebody else. You cannot arm Ajax against the unpredictable flashes of parliamentary lightning. Ajax must have read his papers himself. He must be soaked in his stuff like a good salad is soaked in oil. Now Churchill is not a departmental specialist. He prefers, perhaps, some topics, such as naval topics, to others, partly because of a temperamental dramaticism, partly because, looking back over his life, there is no job of which he can be more proud and in which he was more immersed than getting the Fleet ready between 1911 and 1914. But he does any job with all his might. No detail is too small for a mind infinitely agile and refreshed by his curious habit of going to bed for a couple of hours every afternoon. Moreover, when in one office he generally found time to exhilarate or irritate some of his colleagues by stimulating memoranda on the business of their offices. After all, there is no man who has held more offices himself, and held them for nearly half a century since he first became Colonial Under-Secretary in 1905. Thus he possesses in exceptional measure that experience which is essential to the good parliamentarian.

What is also necessary is to accept without moaning the ups and downs of success and failure which are inseparable from the career. There is, of course, a difference between abstention from moaning and pusillanimous acceptance. Churchill, for example, fought fiercely against the most unmerited setback of his career when the whole odium for the Gallipoli fiasco was shovelled and shuffled on to him; and he had to wait a long time for vindication. But he accepted temporary relegation on this occasion, though deeply wounded, with very considerable dignity, surpassed only by the way in which he accepted the far more surprising ejection from office in 1945. These kinds of somersaults of luck are what parliamentarians must learn to expect. If they have parliamentary institutions in their bones, the somersaults are disliked but not misunderstood nor resented; whereas people of a different temperament, such as Mussolini, or Hitler, or Stalin can neither grasp nor tolerate them. It is tempting, amid the preoccupations of eminence, to slip into a dictatorial attitude, and to feel that the House of Commons can be treated like a rubber-stamp. It is also fatal. Churchill never made that mistake. All through the war he treated both House and people with unfailing respect. Parliament is the thread which has run through his whole life, and it has been a life-line, keeping brilliance in balance.

I do not know whether parliamentary institutions are

destined to be trampled into shapelessness by the feet of young or even middle-aged Leftists in a hurry. They may even be choked by the present fashion of ramming enormous quantities of stuff down their throats. But whether either of these disasters ever happens or not, they will remain as a type of machinery, invented by man for the conduct of human affairs, possessing qualities peculiar to the British race. They are on record as having thrown up during recent centuries a body of men capable of bearing comparison in character and in ability with any who have directed the affairs of any nation at any time. Among these men, Sir Winston Churchill holds an unchallengeable place.

Colin R. Coote.

The Campbell-Bannerman— Asquith Government

by Viscount Samuel

W HEN I came into the House of Commons at a by-election at the end of 1902, Churchill had already been there for two years; at the age of twenty-five he had been elected as Conservative member for Oldham. His father, Lord Randolph Churchill, leader of 'the Fourth Party'—an able group of Tory Democrats in the late Victorian Parliaments—and for a short time Chancellor of the Exchequer and Leader of the House, had been a great political figure in his day. Winston was 'born in the purple', at the very centre of the public life of England, and of a family illustrious in its history. But he was notable not only by lineage. He stood out, from the beginning, as a personality in his own right. He had already served in four military campaigns, and had written four books about them. He had contested two parliamentary elections; defeated in the first, he had tried again in the same constituency, and won. In the House of Commons he was beginning to make his mark as a speaker. Already he was looked upon as a coming man.

It was an exciting moment in the world of politics. There were clear signs of great changes impending. The Conservatives had been in power, under the leadership of Lord Salisbury, for a period of sixteen years, broken only by the short term, precarious and uneasy, of the Gladstone-Rosebery Government. Arthur Balfour had lately succeeded his uncle as head of the Cabinet, now riddled with dissensions. The Conservative Party was split from top to bottom by Joseph Chamberlain's campaign for Protective Tariffs. Against him, some of the ablest of the younger Tories in the House were forming an independent group—the Unionist Free Traders: among them were not only Balfour's relatives, Robert and Hugh Cecil, but also Randolph Churchill's son. With civil war threatening to break out at any moment within their party, this group were tending more and more towards the Liberals.

It was clear that the main issue at the next election would be Free Trade; and no longer the question of Irish Home Rule, which had dominated British politics —except during the South African War—for twenty years. In order to rally all possible forces in a combined attack to oust the Tories from power, the Liberal leaders had decided, with the full concurrence of their Irish Nationalist allies, to hold the Home Rule policy in abeyance; not to include it in the programme for the ensuing general election, but reserve it for consideration in a later Parliament. This greatly eased the position of the Unionist Free Traders—as it was intended to do. It became more and more clear, as the end of the Parliament drew closer, that, when the time came, that group would be found in the Liberal line of battle.

Already the active younger members were beginning to foregather. Here are two brief extracts relating to Winston Churchill, the first from a diary I kept in 1904 —the only time I ever did so—the second from a family letter written soon after:

28 July 1904
Dined at the Bachelors' Club with Murray (the Master of Elibank): 17 there, almost all young Liberal M.P.s. Walked back to the House with Winston Churchill, and we talked of the next Liberal Government, Ireland, redistribution of seats and other things.

3 March 1905
Went to the Speaker's Levée . . . Winston Churchill was there in a cavalry uniform with a long row of medals. He is a most astounding person. His speeches in the House this session have been very fine.

Month by month it was becoming more and more evident that the Government was nearing its end. A number of different factors were turning one section after another of the electorate against the tottering Administration. A continuous series of by-elections— the one at which I had been returned was among the earliest—made plain beyond doubt the way the country was going. At last Balfour resigned; a Liberal Government was formed, with Campbell-Bannerman as Prime Minister; Parliament was dissolved; and at the election the Liberal Party was swept into power with the largest majority since the time of the Great Reform Bill. Among its serried ranks was Winston Churchill, Liberal member for the key constituency of North-west Manchester.

The day after the Liberal Cabinet took office, the newspapers published the list of the new Under-Secretaries. Winston Churchill's name and my own appeared next to one another—he for the Colonies, I for the Home Office. For the next ten years continuously we were to be colleagues in the Ministry.

The post assigned to him was one of special importance at that time. The Colonial Secretary, Lord Elgin, being in the House of Lords, the business of the Department in the Commons was in the charge of the Under-Secretary. And, as South African affairs were still matters of keen controversy and the Colonial Office was the Department directly concerned, it was Churchill who had to bear the brunt of criticism and attack, day by day at Question Time and in the often embittered debates that were constantly arising. This he did— with great distinction, unvarying success, and growing authority. And with zest; for he was, where he always wished to be, in the centre of the firing line.

That in his young days he was ambitious he would have been the last to deny. But his ambitions were legitimate; they were pursued always by honourable means; and, if they were fulfilled it was because they were justified by great talents and sustained by an unremitting industry.

I remember that, not long after our appointment, we were attending some official function; and, as Under-Secretaries, were wearing ministerial uniform of the Second Class, the First Class being for members of the Cabinet and other Privy Councillors: the difference between them is indicated by the gold embroidery on the collar and cuffs having a plain edge for the higher class and a serrated edge for the lower. Winston was by no means pleased at being no more than an Under-Secretary, young as he was and even as a first step in office. Suddenly, pointing to his sleeve he said to me: 'The badge of shame!'

It was not long, however, before he had the unusual distinction of being sworn of the Privy Council while still an Under-Secretary and the badge of shame was soon eliminated. (He is now the senior Privy Councillor.) And in 1908, when the Ministry was reconstructed on Campbell-Bannerman's death, with Asquith as Premier, Churchill entered the Cabinet as President of the Board of Trade. (I followed as Chancellor of the Duchy of Lancaster in the next year.) Soon Churchill was transferred to the Home Office, and, after a short time, began his memorable term of service, in times of strain and of peril, as First Lord of the Admiralty.

In the House of Commons he was a debater of the first order. But he was always chary of speaking unprepared. His speeches—their substance, their arrangement, their phrasing—were then, as they are now, the outcome of much thought and careful reflection. But so full is he of what he proposes to say that, when it comes to be delivered, the speech has all the appearance

—and the effect—of spontaneity. (Very different was this from the parliamentary habits of Lloyd George, who, on most occasions, would intervene in the debate armed with nothing more than two or three half-sheets of notepaper, jotted mostly with references to remarks by previous speakers: and, as often as not, even these would be forgotten, and much of the speech, taking its colour from the temper of the House, would follow lines quite unpremeditated.)

I remember well that on one occasion, some years later, I was sitting on the Front Bench on one side of Mr. Asquith with Winston on the other, when the debate, which was on some important matter, took an unexpected turn. It seemed to the Prime Minister that it had become necessary that Churchill should give the Government reply. Being quite unprepared, this he was most unwilling to do. But, as the debate went on, it became clear that he and no one else must answer. Mr. Asquith pressed it, and in the end Winston rose, obviously disquieted, nervous, and apprehensive. The speech, though short, proved brilliant and effective in a high degree. The House was delighted, the Prime Minister grateful, and Winston himself much relieved.

As a legislator Churchill, in those years, had a great share in carrying on to the statute book the extensive programme of social reform which was the principal objective of that Government. At the Board of Trade he was responsible for two important measures: first, the Bill that established the Labour Exchanges, and so saved unemployed workpeople from a wearisome and sometimes heartbreaking expenditure of time and trouble in going from place to place in search of work; and second, the Trade Boards Bill, which ended once for all the scandals of the Sweating System in home industries. And as Home Secretary he was responsible for the first general measure dealing with the excessive hours of labour in shops and securing to all assistants a weekly half-holiday.

The meetings he addressed in the country attracted great audiences everywhere. His speeches were incisive and uncompromising, but always witty and good tempered; arousing the enthusiasm of his supporters without stirring too much the resentment of his opponents. He was a tower of strength to the Government in its perpetual hard campaigning in the constituencies.

In the Cabinet, Churchill's leading position in the House of Commons and in the country lent weight to his views. Surprisingly, among all our colleagues it was with Lloyd George that, from the beginning, he was most closely associated. Their backgrounds had been so different, and they were believed to approach the great group of questions relating to the Empire, defence, and foreign policy from standpoints so wide apart that we had not expected to find such intimate co-operation between them in all their plans and policies. Lloyd George was the most active protagonist of the social reform policy; it was fortunate that he was able to enlist a partner so keen and effective as Churchill proved to be.

This partnership held fast even when, in 1909, an acute division of opinion about the Navy threatened the solidarity of the Cabinet. The question was how far the Fleet would have to be strengthened in order to meet the threat from the rapid expansion of the German Navy. The main point was the right programme for the new battleship class of Dreadnoughts; should there be four, or six, or eight, and how quickly must they be built. Lloyd George, newly established at the Exchequer and planning his great social reform Budget, was opposing any larger expenditure than was absolutely essential and would not agree to more than four; Churchill supported him. McKenna, at the Admiralty, and a large and powerful section of the Cabinet, insisted upon six. A strong body of opinion in Parliament and in the country carried on a campaign with the slogan: 'We want eight and we won't wait.' In the end, it was this policy to which, after much struggle and stress and risk of resignations, the Cabinet agreed. As Churchill put it in his *World Crisis*, 'a curious and characteristic solution was reached. The Admiralty had demanded six ships: the economists offered four, and we finally compromised on eight.' This had been reached by some concessions on both sides as to the timing of the construction.

But, two years later, when the international situation had suddenly become critical through the provocative action of Germany in what was known as 'the Agadir incident', Mr. Asquith arranged unexpectedly an exchange of offices between McKenna, the First Lord, and Churchill, the Home Secretary. By that time Churchill had become fully convinced of the need for the maximum strengthening of the Fleet, and devoted himself thenceforth to that task with what an historian has described as 'feverish activity'.

Then came the supreme crisis of July 1914. Again

the Cabinet was deeply divided, reflecting a division, which seemed likely to be unbridgeable, in the Liberal Party, both in the Commons and in the country. It seemed at one moment that a third of our number might resign. Lloyd George's attitude remained uncertain until almost the last moment. Churchill's was never in doubt. He stood with Asquith, Grey, and Haldane in holding that this country would find itself bound, if not at once then certainly in the end, to support France in resisting the German aggression, and that its intervention could only be effective if it was immediate. But when Germany finally invaded Belgium, and the Belgians resisted, Britain's treaty obligation to support the Belgians in precisely that eventuality came into the forefront. The duty was undeniable and unescapable, and the Cabinet, with two exceptions—John Morley and John Burns—was at one. Britain faced its great ordeal with a united Government, and, because of that, with a united people.

In that terrible war Winston Churchill rendered great services to his country. But in the second war that was to come twenty years after, his services were destined to be even greater, for he was the acknowledged leader of the whole nation at a moment when the peril itself was greater—exceeding any in all the long annals of the British people.

Few are left now of those who knew him and worked with him in the early days. But all know him—here and the world over—as he became in later years, and as he is now.

There is a charming story of Marshal Joffre, in his old age, and a little girl to whom he was presenting a prize on the school prize-day. He said some words of congratulation, to which the child answered, with a curtsey, '*C'est un grand honneur, mon maréchal, de vous revoir.*' '*Tiens, ma petite, tu m'as déja rencontré?*' '*Dans l'histoire, mon maréchal.*'

There, everyone meets Winston Churchill, and will meet him through the generations—in History.

Samuel

Two Great War Leaders

by THE RT. HON. L. S. AMERY

Twice in the lifetime of our generation has England faced the ordeal of a struggle for her very existence. Twice her good fortune has found, at the critical hour, a leader who could inspire her people and direct their energies through defeat to crowning victory, a pilot who knew how to weather the storm. How did those tasks compare, and how did those leaders themselves compare with each other in their quality of leadership? History alone can give the final answer to that question. But one who was privileged to work in close contact with both during those great years can at least bring out some of the more striking resemblances and differences between the men themselves, their methods and their circumstances.

Both were self-made men, though in very different senses of the word. Lloyd George, after a boyhood spent in the humble, but cultured, home of a Welsh shoemaker, began his career as a local solicitor. His ardent and eloquent championship of Welsh Nonconformity against the then dominant Anglican Church, and of Welsh tenants against Anglicized landlords,

brought him into Parliament. His sympathy for the
Boers first won him notoriety. His eloquence and his
local influence assured office when the Liberals were
returned in 1906. At the Board of Trade and then at
the Treasury he soon proved that he was something
much more than an aggressive platform orator and an
adroit debater. His imaginative, constructive radicalism
gave new life to a Liberal Party which had lost its
original meaning and momentum. War and its problems had never crossed his horizon, and when the
issue presented itself in August 1914 he first shrank
from it. Once the decision was taken the whole restless
energy of his nature was thrown into the task of overcoming the unimaginative obstruction of the Departments and the inertia of his Prime Minister. In so far
as there was any leadership in the first two years of the
war he gave it, or tried to give it, and his achievement
in those years must go to his credit in an assessment of
his part in winning the war.

Churchill was born in the heart of that inner circle
which, eighty years ago, still led society and directed
policy. From the first he could afford to set his targets
high. He did so with conscious purpose, modelling
himself upon the men whose careers most deeply impressed his imagination. There was the military ideal,
embodied for the young soldier in the mighty personality of Napoleon, offering immediate adventure in
the minor warfare of that age, but, so it then seemed,
little scope for real greatness—a shadowy ideal rather
than a practical aim. There was the political target,
embodied in the meteoric rise to fame and power of
Lord Randolph Churchill, and the challenge to filial

piety to make good, where a father had fallen beyond recovery. For a decade and more the young politician shaped himself to that model, fighting against Service estimates and avenging his father upon the party which had so incontinently dropped him. With charge of the Navy in face of the growing German menace the ideal of leadership in war revived. Actual war brought bitter disappointment, but, with it, the sobering lesson that strategy, however brilliant or sound—and Antwerp and the Dardanelles were both—is useless without the power to see it through. The post-war years found him back in the Conservative camp and, presently, in his father's office of Chancellor of the Exchequer. Once again he seemed bent on following in his father's footsteps, not only in policy, but in the increasing estrangement between himself and the party which he had rejoined. For ten years he was in the wilderness and seemed to have fallen, 'like Lucifer, never to hope again'.

It was in those years that, at last, he found his true model. In his great ancestor, Marlborough, he discovered that fusion of political and military ideals, as well as the inspiration of family piety, for which he had all his life been groping. To the practical conduct of military affairs in the field and in the administration of Navy, Army, Air Force, and Munitions, he now added a deeper insight into the handling by a master mind of the complex whole of a great crisis in which the management of home and allied politics, the march of armies and their deployment on the field of battle, all played their indispensable part in saving the freedom of Europe. Before the work was finished, what was begun as an historical study and a vindication by a fallen statesman, became the preparation, by the nation's destined future leader, for a new struggle transcending all that had gone before in its long history. When the call came he could truly say of himself, 'I felt as if I were walking with destiny and that all my past life had been but a preparation for this hour and for this trial,' and could justifiably add, 'I thought I knew a good deal about it all.'

Between Churchill and Lloyd George there was all the difference between the trained master of the art of war and the gifted and imaginative amateur. But the difference extended in no less degree to the two nations they were called upon to lead. England in 1914 had not known major war for a century. Neither the nation as a whole, nor its statesmen, nor the professional leaders of its fighting services, had any conception of the scale or intensity of the effort that would be demanded. Lloyd George's greatness lay in the creative energy which overcame the dead weight of obstructive resistance in every field before the nation was fully geared to war. Even so it was only towards the very end that anything in the nature of an Allied strategic direction of the war was secured, and that long after events had precluded any freedom of strategic action. The England of 1940 had, in a moment, dropped all the wishful illusions of the inter-war years, and was back where 1918 left off, ready to accept all the measures the necessity for which had been proved by the Great Rehearsal of the First War. Somewhat rusty in parts, but essentially intact, the great engine of national war only needed expansion and brave direction. Not only Churchill, but the nation 'knew a good deal about it all', and was ready to entrust its fate to one who both knew and had foreseen.

If Lloyd George shrank from the issue of war, once that issue was decided he was for victory heart and soul. His swift resolution in the opening days averted a financial crisis. Within a few weeks he was pressing the need for sufficient munitions, a battle he carried on for months against the stubborn obstructiveness of Kitchener and the War Office till the 'shell scandal' in May 1915 brought about the first Coalition and made him Minister of Munitions. Now, at last, he was in a position to improvise an organization by methods and on a scale hitherto undreamt of. But only by resolutely brushing aside War Office obstruction. Typical of his methods was the interview in which he made Kitchener initial his statement that four machine guns per battalion were a maximum and anything more a luxury. Going back to his office he told Sir Eric Geddes to square the four, then double and then double again. It was not long before thirty-two per battalion was the normal figure, and, by the end of the war, the supply at the front or in reserve in France stood at sixty-four per battalion. In the ten months between the outbreak of war and June 1915 the War Office had ordered 1,792 machine guns. By the end of the war the Ministry which Lloyd George created had produced 240,000. When the War Office rejected the Stokes Mortar Lloyd George financed its development from a private fund. With Churchill he pressed for tanks, overcoming Haig's initial contempt for this unsoldierly substitute for cavalry, and then in vain trying to prevent their premature partial use. It was not only the War Office that created difficulties.

Labour was no less unprepared to adjust itself to the national need. No small part of Lloyd George's energies and eloquence had to be devoted to settling strikes and to appealing for better work and against the growing mischief of drink.

Soon it became obvious that more men would be needed, as well as more weapons, and that voluntary service could no longer supply them. From the spring of 1915 onwards Lloyd George was pleading in Cabinet, backed by Conservatives like Curzon, against most of his Liberal colleagues, for compulsory service. But even then his whole nature revolted against the wasting of life in futile attacks upon the fortified German line in France. As early as January 1915 he was urging, in a remarkable memorandum, the immense opportunity offered by using our growing forces to rally all the armies of the Balkan countries on our side for the destruction of the ramshackle Austro-Hungarian and Ottoman Empires. It was an essentially sound plan, and might well have secured automatically, or at least greatly helped, what Churchill tried to secure by the opening of the Dardanelles. But there he was up against soldiers whose whole horizon was limited to the Western Front, or rather to the British section of that front, and could only see, in any suggestion of a wider strategy, a 'sideshow' impairing the prospects of the only victory in which they were interested.

Such sideshows still took place, first at the Dardanelles under Churchill's impetuous insistence, and then, when for want of proper support, Gallipoli was abandoned, at Salonika; but only when Serbia was crushed and all hope of rallying the Balkans had faded out. They represented no strategy of any kind; only the conflicting pull of differing personalities in a Cabinet without leadership either in the political or in the military sphere. Convinced that the central machinery for conducting the war was itself unfit for its task and in unfit hands, Lloyd George was driven to a demand for changes which resulted, after a few days of confused intrigue, in his finding himself Prime Minister, at the head of a mixed coalition consisting of part of his own party and of the Conservative minority whose chiefs had, most of them till the last moment, been opposed to his leadership, and who, as a body, still looked upon him with suspicion. With this lukewarm support he had to cope with the resentful hostility of the main body of Asquith's followers, with the Irish and a large part of Labour and, not least, with the deep distrust of the soldiers who knew him as a scathing critic of their methods and of their cherished strategy. As for the nation, it had no doubt admired his eloquence and energy as displayed in public. It knew nothing of the unwearied effort and the constant warning which had preceded his assumption of so fateful a responsibility.

His first task was to create his instrument of Government. A War Cabinet of five replaced what he contemptuously called a 'Sanhedrin', while the machinery of the Committee of Imperial Defence, with the invaluable Sir Maurice (Lord) Hankey in charge, was taken over, lock, stock, and barrel, in order to provide, what no Cabinet had ever had before, a secretariat, not only to record its decisions but to see to their execution. With Milner as his right-hand man and pivot of the whole organization, and with colleagues of the ability of Bonar Law, Curzon, and presently Smuts, this was a body capable both of supervising and co-ordinating the complex machinery of administration as a whole, and also of agreeing, in more intimate discussion, upon the broader issues of war policy. One other mind, indeed, that could have contributed much was absent. But political and military prejudice combined to keep Churchill out of the picture at the outset, and only yielded with vehemently outspoken reluctance to his being employed at all in the, by then, relatively minor post of Minister of Munitions.

It was not long before the new Government was faced with the gravest crisis of the whole war. By bringing the United States into the war the German unrestricted submarine campaign no doubt assured ultimate victory. But only our own efforts could prevent the complete breakdown of our national life, as well as of our war effort, long before any effective help could come from across the Atlantic. And those efforts would have been utterly inadequate if Lloyd George had not overcome the stubborn resistance of the Admiralty to the convoy system which saved the situation.

There was one resistance, indeed, which Lloyd George could not overcome, at least until narrow escape from disaster made it possible for him to achieve his main purpose. That was the resistance of Haig and Robertson, not only to any operations other than on the French front, but to any unity of strategic direction even on that front. It was not only that he lacked that unquestioning confidence in his own judgment which could have enabled him to override and, if necessary, supersede Haig and Robertson, rather than assent to the wasteful slaughter of Passchendaele. It was the knowledge that the men who were his military advisers had the ear of influential elements both in the Conservative Party and in the Opposition, and were steadily and unscrupulously working against him. In the end he got his way by roundabout means, first by securing alternative advice, framed from a wider point of view, through the establishment of the Inter-Allied Supreme War Council and its military staff dominated by Henry Wilson, then, after Haig and Pétain's obstinacy had all but lost the situation, by the setting up of the United Command under Foch. Even so, it was only by bringing Wilson and Milner into the War Office that he achieved for the last six months that complete unity of military and political direction which Churchill enjoyed from the outset.

Very different were the conditions under which Churchill took command. After all his warnings, no one could gainsay his moral right to the position. No bitterness, no suggestion of intrigue, had attended his displacing Chamberlain whom he had loyally defended to the end. He had no real Opposition to contend with, from the first day to the last, but at most occasional individual criticism of particular policies. When Neville Chamberlain resigned he strengthened his position still further by becoming leader of the Conservative Party.

Nor could any one, least of all the chiefs of the fighting services, dispute his qualifications. None of them could claim a comparable all-round knowledge of war in all its aspects, or a more profound study of its history. What is more, he was for all of them not only a politician, but one of themselves, one who could see their problems from their own point of view, who could think their thoughts and speak their language. If he advocated some daring strategical move they remembered that he had been right both about Antwerp and about the Dardanelles. If he commended some imaginative technical device for their consideration they might recall his advocacy of the tank or even, just possibly, of an earlier scheme for a Mulberry harbour off the Frisian Islands. He was their master, and they knew it. They might differ on some particular point. But they trusted his general judgment.

Churchill, for his part, had much better reason to accept theirs than Lloyd George had. The First Sea Lord, Pound, was an old and trusted friend. Dill and Alan Brooke, who successively held the post of Chief of the Imperial General Staff, were men of a quite different calibre and breadth of outlook from Haig and Robertson. Portal, the Chief of the Air Staff, embodied in himself and in his duties, both a wider purview and a link between the Services lacking in the rudimentary Air Service of the First World War. What is more, the Chiefs of Staff Committee, as such, had long provided the elementary machinery for a more comprehensive study of strategical problems. By the bold stroke of making himself Minister of Defence, Churchill attached the Chiefs of Staff to his own person for all purposes of strategy, and, by the further device of annexing their Planning section, secured for himself the initiative in the formulation of all war plans. In effect he divided the War Cabinet into two halves, a strategical Cabinet consisting of himself and the Chiefs of Staff, with General Ismay as Secretary, and a Cabinet of general policy, with Sir E. Bridges as Secretary, over which he presided, but to which he readily delegated most current administrative and domestic problems. Where Lloyd George had to defend his view against the Service Chiefs in front of colleagues, some of whom were by no means always in agreement with him, Churchill had only to inform the War Cabinet of what he and the Chiefs of Staff had already agreed among themselves. They were, as a rule, well content, and with good reason.

Lloyd George's methods reflected the general improvisation which marked the earlier war and the multifariousness of the tasks with which he had to grapple, as well as his own personal character. His uncertain moiety of the Liberal Party, the more important members of the Conservative Party and, not least, the Press, had to be kept together. A continuous series of breakfast parties provided the most convenient instrument for this, as well as for unofficial meetings with anyone who had a new idea to contribute, or for squaring a difficult colleague before the daily War Cabinet meeting. He loved stir and bustle, and, for all his conviction of the necessity for a small Cabinet, was never so happy as when the Cabinet room was filled to overflowing, or when he could play the leading part at a crowded international conference. He could compose occasional effective memoranda. But, as a rule, he put little on paper, whether by his own pen or by dictation. With a memory only too prone to be affected by his outlook at the moment that was apt to create difficulties.

Churchill, on the contrary, contributed both to the avoidance of misunderstandings at the time and to historical knowledge hereafter by that continuous stream of dictated 'directives', some, in fact, definite orders, others more in the nature of stimulating suggestions, which he has since appended to his War Memoirs. His hours were both early and late. The early hours were spent in bed dealing with all the day's news, issuing directives, and preparing for the morning's meeting with the Chiefs of Staff. A long rest in the afternoon prepared him for the remainder of the day's work, including Cabinet meetings, often beginning after ten in the evening and followed by the drafting and discussion of important telegrams. Where Lloyd George, a much younger man, could be busy talking with one person or another all day, Churchill wisely husbanded his strength for the greatness of the decisions which had to be taken.

At Cabinet meetings, indeed, Lloyd George spoke relatively little, at any rate at the outset. For one thing, there were so many problems to settle, and it was essential to secure agreement by finding out what others thought, a process which Lloyd George enjoyed, and to which he brought an almost superhuman sensitiveness. For another, the opinions of those colleagues mattered more, both in themselves and in their political effect. For yet another, the methodical Hankey was at his side, ever concerned with getting through the agenda. A Churchill Cabinet was primarily an opportunity for the Prime Minister to tell his colleagues what was happening, what he thought about it, and how he meant to deal with it, followed by as much of the agenda as time allowed. Each method was immensely interesting and effectively served its purpose. But one

could wish that some of Churchill's discourses could
have been recorded for the benefit of posterity. Most
memorable of these talks was one given to all his colleagues of Cabinet rank at the time of the Dunkirk
evacuation, when he told us that we could hardly hope
to save more than forty-five thousand men, and, after
surveying all the consequences, added that whatever
else happened we should, of course, fight on. My mind
went back to what was once said of the great Chatham,
that no one ever 'left his Cabinet without feeling himself
a braver man'.

No situation, indeed, that ever confronted Lloyd
George was quite so terrible as that which Churchill
had to face after Dunkirk and the collapse of France.
The possibility of that collapse, and, with it, that of
Italy, was actually envisaged by Lloyd George in the
summer of 1918. But by then America was in the war,
the submarine menace had been mastered and invasion
from the air was not yet a possibility. We might not
have won in Europe. But we could not have been defeated. And the rest of the world was ours. Where
Churchill's achievement stands pre-eminent is in the
courageous weighing of risks which, when all Western
Europe was in German hands, and invasion imminent,
yet sent all our armour round the Cape to Egypt and
enabled Wavell to win the victories which saved the
Middle East. The loss of the Middle East, and with it
of most of Africa, might well have decided the United
States that we were done and not worth rescuing. No
less was the courage which took the chance of endan-
gering success in the Middle East by that intervention
in Greece which, unsuccessful in itself, saved Moscow

and wrecked the German airborne division which might otherwise have secured Iraq against us.

One end at which Lloyd George aimed from the first was a united Allied strategy and, on the Western Front, at least, a united command. Working against the fierce resistance of the soldiers, and with ever-changing French governments, he only secured his object towards the very end. Churchill, so far at least as the United States were concerned, found no obstacles either from Roosevelt or from either British or American Commanders in securing effective strategical co-operation at the top, or the loyal acceptance of a unified command in each theatre of war. He had, indeed, to contend, in the case of the Americans, with the same prepossession for the frontal attack upon the enemy's main force that Lloyd George had to meet from Haig and Robertson. But he got enough of his way to prevent an attempt to rush the Western Front in 1943, an attempt which might well have been far more costly than Passchendaele, and wholly disastrous.

No one, in a democratic country like ours, can be a great war leader who has not the gift of inspired and inspiring utterance. Lloyd George was a natural orator whose speeches owed far less to preparation than to the response of the audience before him. They served his purpose admirably in dealing with difficult industrial audiences, as well as with great popular demonstrations or with a crowded House of Commons. But they were essentially for the occasion. Churchill's oratory is of a very different type. It is the result of the transformation, by long years of effort and practice, of a purely literary rhetoric into an eloquence as easy as it is lofty; an eloquence as effective over the wireless or in cold print as to his immediate audience. It served him, not only to voice the stubborn courage of the nation, but to inspire it with a deeper sense of its own history and to give it a nobler quality. Nor was it limited to his own people here and beyond the seas. Through all the long years of German Occupation countless secret listeners, from Norway to Greece, were encouraged in their resistance, or at least sustained in their faith, by the unshakable confidence in that strong mellow voice. There are passages in Churchill's speeches which will remain a lasting addition to our literature. But on that theme other contributors to this volume will have written more fully.

Demosthenes once described the supreme quality and purpose of oratory as action. Both Lloyd George and Churchill were, above all, restless men of action for whom eloquence was only an instrument, and not an end in itself. Both were men of undaunted courage: Lloyd George the more swiftly resilient; Churchill more grimly and imperturbably resolute. Both, like Odysseus, masters of device; the one snatching ideas from the atmosphere of the moment; the other drawing upon a long accumulated store of thought on the problems of war. In most other respects their characters and temperaments were in striking contrast.

Lloyd George's mind, like his career, was discontinuous in regard both to time and to ideas. He had, indeed, his local patriotism for Wales and the Welsh language. But no broader background of history and tradition, even as regards the principles of that Liberal Party into which he was born. His mind was, indeed, too quick and too open both to new ideas and to those of his political opponents to allow of any rigid consistency with any set of principles or with his own past. It was a mind of disconcerting agility. Lord Milner once said to me after a Cabinet meeting that the only thing like it was the knight on the chessboard—it moved in two different directions simultaneously, both unexpected. So quick was he in taking up the ideas of others that a favourite jest in the First World War was that the country was governed by two men, Lloyd George and the last person he had spoken to—a valuable quality in breaking through hierarchical obscurantism in the Departments, but not always conducive to good results or good feeling. In his eagerness to get things done, in his absorption in the ideas and methods of the immediate occasion, and in his complete forgetfulness of what he had thought or said before, he created an impression of clever unscrupulousness and intrigue which did not do him justice. He was the consummate natural actor who lived wholeheartedly in the part of the moment, with little thought for other parts he may have played before.

In all this Churchill is the very opposite. Born into a great family with a famous history and at the heart of England's ruling class, he imbibed from Gibbon and Macaulay that profound and vivid sense both of the fateful movement and of the romantic pageant of the history of nations and of Empires which has dominated his outlook. To play his part in that great drama was his natural and mastering ambition. Not any part that came along, but the particular part of leadership in some secular crisis; to reincarnate his great ancestor,

or Chatham, or the younger Pitt; to stand out in history
as the champion of English freedom against another
Philip of Spain, or Louis XIV, or Napoleon. Mean-
while to make his mark in the politics of the day, as
early as possible with that great end in view. That
dramatic sense of historic continuity has not been
accompanied by Lloyd George's instinct for, and even
anticipation of, the movement of contemporary thought.
The supreme moments of history are outside the fluc-
tuations of political opinion, and at such a moment he
could truly interpret the heart and mind of his countrymen and of the Empire as no one else could have done.
At other times he has often seemed to belong to another
and earlier generation.

With this difference in intellectual outlook has gone
a corresponding difference in their relations to those
with whom they have had to work. Churchill has always
been too full of his own original thought-world, too
self-contained, to be much affected by the thoughts of
others or to be even conscious of them, except, on
occasion, as resistances to be overborne by force of
argument and eloquence. Lloyd George had an almost
uncanny faculty of sensing what others thought and felt,
even before they knew it themselves, and of entering into
their thoughts and feelings in order to assimilate them
or else divert them by persuasion into the desired channel. There never was any man who lived so entirely by
immediate reaction to his surroundings. I sometimes
felt that if he had been placed in a completely empty
whitewashed room he would, like a character in one of
Henry James's stories, have disintegrated and dissolved
into nothing. Churchill, in such a situation, might im-

perturbably continue rehearsing the next speech or the next chapter, or, if aware of the bare walls, seize upon the opportunity for the expression of his talent as a painter.

Each served the needs of his occasion. Only Lloyd George's driving impulse and power of all-round improvisation could have coped with the general unreadiness and confusion of the First World War. Only Churchill's trained knowledge and wealth of historic inspiration have matched the height of his achievement in the Second. Lloyd George rose to greatness kindled by the stress of circumstances as he found himself confronted by them. For Churchill the great event came, and found him prepared to shape it for his country's saving, prepared as no British Prime Minister before him; ready 'to serve, full harnessed as of old, the days that are the destinies'.

Ss Amery

Across the House

by THE RT. HON. C. R. ATTLEE

SIR WINSTON CHURCHILL's parliamentary career
has now extended over fifty-four years. I can only
judge the first twenty-two years by hearsay, but he
must have been great fun in his early and quite irres-
ponsible days. He was, too, in the thick of all the party
fights before the First World War, gladly giving and
taking hard knocks.

In 1924 he returned to the House of Commons as
Chancellor of the Exchequer. As a very junior ex-
Under-Secretary, it was not for me to cross swords
with him, but I used to enjoy his contests with his opposite number, Philip Snowden, whose acidity was an
admirable foil to Churchill's more boisterous methods.
Every Budget provided the opportunity for a full-dress
fight between them. I have often wondered how Members of Parliament in the past could have been en-
thralled by Mr. Gladstone's Budget speeches. I seldom
find Budget speeches exciting and I have had to listen
to a great many, though I admired the lucidity of
Stafford Cripps. Churchill's Budget speeches were

always interesting. It was exciting to speculate which henroost he would rob next and how ingeniously he would do it.

I learned in that Parliament of 1924 what a master he was in the art of answering Parliamentary Questions. He could deliver a knock-out blow or give the retort courteous with equal facility. I recall a reply from those days. Jack Jones, who often scored bull's-eyes at Question Time, for once made a bad shot. Came the retort, 'I have often heard the Honourable Member do much better than that.' One never can anticipate just what line he will take, except that it will generally be effective.

During the war it was often my duty to take the Prime Minister's Questions at short notice. I often had to seek hurriedly for an alteration in some witty reply to a Conservative which would not have been very acceptable from me.

Although I think that Sir Winston Churchill prefers making set speeches after careful preparation, he is a master at improvisation. I recall one occasion when he was defeated. He had to reply to a debate and we knew that he had nothing to say, but we knew also that if he could provoke interventions from our side, he would get away with it. Mr. Shinwell and I managed to persuade all our Members to remain silent. In vain he trailed his coat. There was no response and he ran out of matter.

The next phase that I recall is the period when he was at odds with his party and took a seat on the Bench below the Gangway on the Government side. Here he was well placed to fire on both parties. I remember describing him as a heavily armed tank cruising in No Man's Land.

Very impressive were the speeches he delivered as the international horizon grew darker. He became very unpopular with the predominant group in his own party, but he never minded fighting a lone battle.

In 1940 his hour of destiny struck. The time had come when his particular qualities were needed. He was fortunate to have his chance, but the country was still more fortunate to have him. No one who heard them will ever forget those great speeches in which he divined and gave expression to the resolve of the whole nation. I always admired the skill with which he would find the right setting in his speeches for those vivid phrases which he struck out white hot from the anvil of his mind. He was, I think, at his best when he spoke as the leader of the nation.

In the last phase I have had to face him as my opposite number. I doubt if he really cared much for the everyday work of the Leader of the Opposition in the House. He had been too long away from this kind of trench warfare. Curiously enough, he has never mastered the procedure of the House. He gives the impression that anyway the rules don't apply to him. He is far happier as Prime Minister. In these days a Prime Minister is not expected to sit for long hours on the Treasury Bench for this duty falls to the Leader of the House. In the cut and thrust of debate, Sir Winston can deal many shrewd blows, but is stronger in reply than in attack for, when attacking, he is apt to leave a good many openings for ripostes. I would say that he was not the equal of Lloyd George in attack, though excelling him in speeches where a wide sweep over great issues is needed. He rises to the occasion when he is engaged on a lofty theme though no one enjoys more a bit of knock-about when the House is in lighter mood.

He has ever been a generous opponent, quite ready to pay tribute to an opponent even when he has himself been attacked. He can at times be annoyed and rattled, but generally he comes up again smiling a little later. He is to-day the only member of the House who can make a speech in the classical style. The carefully prepared and lengthy oration has rather died out. Asquith, Austen Chamberlain, and Lloyd George were in the old tradition, but debate nowadays has become more conversational. Churchill is the last of the giants surviving from the Victorian era.

C. R. Attlee

Churchill and the Navy

by ADMIRAL OF THE FLEET LORD FRASER
OF NORTH CAPE

So much has been said, seen, and written of Sir Winston Churchill that these few lines can be no more than a small tribute from an ordinary sailor—who, as Controller of the Navy, had the pleasure and privilege of serving under him when he was First Lord of the Admiralty, and of working with him more indirectly when he was Prime Minister and Minister of Defence.

Just prior to the war the Admiralty suffered in their higher ranks. My predecessor died in office and there was an interval of some two months before I took his place in March 1939. Shortly afterwards the First Sea Lord, Sir Roger Backhouse, was taken ill and died, leaving a further gap before his successor, Sir Dudley Pound, could move in. It was in such circumstances that sometime in the summer of that year I went with my Director of Scientific Research, Professor Wright, to a meeting of the Anti-Aircraft Research Committee.

Mr. Churchill, as he of course then was, was a member of the Committee, although not in the Government, and for the first time I found myself facing the great man across a table—a little alarming for anyone, but especially for a junior Flag Officer only recently in office. I felt sure that he had something in store for me. Presently he looked across and said: 'Admiral, what is the Navy doing about radar?' Now at that time radar had been kept so secret that few serving Naval officers knew much about it—and very wisely so. However he must have realized my position, for when I could not give him a clear answer he just said in his courteous and kindly way: 'Well, Admiral, it is very important.' That was enough.

On our way back to the Admiralty Professor Wright said: 'I am sorry, Controller, I should have kept you better informed.' 'Not at all,' I replied, 'it is my responsibility; but from now on we must give first priority to the practical side of fitting radar in ships.' We had, of course, a number of able officers working on the problem, but to make any real progress a high degree of priority—especially in finance—was essential. In all such important matters the degree of secrecy to be maintained is always a problem: the wider the circle of knowledge, the quicker the progress but the greater the danger of leakage. Although at the beginning of the war no ships were actually fitted with radar, the policy adopted had probably paid us because we were, and remained, ahead of the Germans. In this matter the Navy owes a great deal to Sir Winston Churchill.

On the outbreak of war we learnt who our new First Lord was. No one on the Board of Admiralty will forget our first Board Meeting. As he once again took the First Lord's chair in the famous Board Room, Churchill was filled with emotion. To a few words of welcome from the First Sea Lord he replied by saying what a privilege and honour it was to be again in that chair, that there were many difficulties ahead but together we would overcome them. He surveyed critically each one of us in turn and then, adding that he would see us all personally later on, he adjourned the meeting, 'Gentlemen,' he said, 'to your tasks and duties.'

The inspiration of a man like Churchill at the head of Admiralty affairs was a revelation to us all. A war room had already been set up, in which the position of the fleets, convoys, and ships were plotted and kept up to date every twelve hours. Captain Pim, R.N.V.R., was appointed in charge and ran it, I think throughout the war, with four or five young R.N.V.R. lieutenants who were unfit for sea service. To them we owe a great debt of gratitude. Each morning at 8 a.m. Captain Pim had to report the news to the First Lord, and this continued after Sir Winston became Prime Minister. It did not matter if the Prime Minister were in his bath at that hour, the path of duty continued uninterrupted. This room was indeed a remarkable institution, and Sir Winston greatly increased its scope. Later, with the help of Lloyds, the position of every merchant ship in the world was plotted; as a result, a cruiser in, say, the South Atlantic, on sighting a merchant ship, could ask the Admiralty whether that ship was in its correct area and on its lawful occasion— and a reply would be sent within half an hour.

The First Lord also devised special red labels with

just three words printed on them: 'Action this day.'
This ensured that any important document on which he
wanted immediate information would be dealt with
at once, and the reply was expected to be on not more
than 'one sheet of paper'. One day, standing by his
desk, a somewhat unorthodox thought came to me;
I surreptitiously put two of these labels in my pocket.
There was a very urgent paper of my own to get
through and with this incentive it came back to me that
same night. Whether Sir Winston came to hear of
this I don't know, but a week later the colour of the
labels was altered and I still carry the remaining label
in my pocket book. Anyway, it is a sound maxim of
war—'Never do the same thing twice.'

Churchill stayed in his Victoria Street flat for some
time after he became First Lord. It was simply fur-
nished and adorned with his own beautiful paintings.
One evening, the Director of Naval Construction, Sir
Stanley Goodall, and I were invited to dine with him
in order to discuss the shipbuilding programme. He
had a high opinion of the D.N.C. whom he had asked,
some time before, to design a machine for digging
trenches. His specification was, I think, a trench six
feet deep by three feet wide at the rate of one mile an
hour. It was a tall order, but a model was made and
demonstrated in the Admiralty—though a change in
the state of the war precluded further development of
the idea. On this particular evening, towards the end of
dinner the telephone rang. When the butler came in,
Sir Winston, who rather disliked telephones, said:
'Who is it?'

'I don't know, sir,' said the butler.

'Well, say I can't attend to it now.'

'I think you ought to come, sir,' said the butler, and Churchill got up rather testily. Then we heard his replies, 'Yes, sir . . . No, sir.' There are few people whom he would address as 'sir' and we wondered who on earth it could be. Presently he came back, evidently much moved, and said: 'Do you know who that was? The President of the United States.' He went on, 'It is remarkable to think of being rung up in this little flat in Victoria Street by the President himself in the midst of a great war.' The telephone conversation was on some question concerning the *Athenia* incident. The First Lord said: 'Admiral, I think you must now excuse me. This is very important and I must go and see the Prime Minister at once.' It may be that this was the beginning of the communications between the President and the 'Former Naval Person'.

Lady Churchill was invited to launch the aircraft carrier *Indomitable*; a ship with such a name seemed a suitable one for the wife of the First Lord to christen and we all travelled to Barrow. I recall Churchill's mood on that occasion—his cheers as the ship was launched, and then the grave salute in realization of the fierce engagements that he knew she would have to face in the future. For one of Churchill's great characteristics is his thought for others, particularly in danger, difficulty, and adversity.

I well remember the *Indomitable*, particularly her part in that famous Malta convoy of August 1942 when the Fleet beat off the attacks of German and Italian shore-based aircraft during a day and a half.

The *Indomitable* was hit on the evening of the second day and disappeared from view in a welter of smoke and spray. We thought she had gone. A moment later, through the dense cloud, a dim light flashed the laconic signal: 'Ready for 25 knots.'

At lunch that day at Barrow, the First Lord said he thought there would soon have to be a Ministry of Defence which he might have to lead. He said he was trying to see how he could manage this whilst still remaining at the Admiralty which he hated the idea of leaving. However, he was soon to become Prime Minister as well as Minister of Defence so there was no option. On his departure from the Admiralty we said a very sad good-bye to this great man who had already done so much in so short a time. As Prime Minister he still kept in close touch with everyone he had known so well at the Admiralty.

One Saturday when he was Prime Minister I was invited down to Chequers and told to bring my ship-building programme with me. The only other Service guest was Lord Portal, then Sir Charles Portal, A.O.C.-in-C. Bomber Command at Uxbridge. It was dark when I arrived. Lady Churchill had gone out visiting hospitals in the neighbourhood. This was the period when the air-raids were in full swing, and when by 8 p.m. his wife had still not returned the Prime Minister was becoming more and more anxious.

'What a stupid thing to do, to be out late like this and no one knows where she is,' he said, striding up and down the room in his zip 'siren-suit'. Rather a case of the pot calling the kettle black, I thought! However, Lady Churchill arrived a few minutes later, and as a minor explosion seemed about to occur we deemed it best to retire, although everyone appeared at dinner in the best of spirits. I suppose there are few more devoted couples in the world than Sir Winston and Lady Churchill and it was easy to appreciate his anxiety. After dinner, photographs of Chequers and its surroundings just taken from the air for identification purposes were put on a screen. To our amazement, in one of them was a large semi-circle of ploughed land about five miles away with a broad arrow in the centre pointing straight at Chequers! The Prime Minister chuckled: 'Look how well I am looked after! But we had better make inquiries in the morning.' On investigation, the strange marking was found to be quite fortuitous; owing to the nature of the ground and obstructing trees the farmer had to plough his land in this fashion. After this, we were presented with an illuminated copy of President Roosevelt's famous message which the Prime Minister treasured so much and which he signed for us. It bears repeating:

> Sail on, O Ship of State!
> Sail on, O Union, strong and great!
> Humanity with all its fears,
> With all the hopes of future years,
> Is hanging breathless on thy fate!

The P.M., Sir Charles, and I then started our meeting. We discussed every conceivable subject. The shipbuilding programme, the building of aircraft, the tactics to be employed, etc. Telephone calls were coming through indicating heavy bomber attacks on

London and about half-past eleven the P.M. said: 'I must go outside to see what is happening.' In the somewhat chilly night we walked across the garden to the Terrace. It was a sorry spectacle. The guns were still in action and many fires were burning, seemingly all round the horizon. The P.M. murmured: 'Poor old London. I should be there.' It was again so symbolic of his thought for others and the feeling that he should be sharing the danger of his fellow citizens. We went back indoors and continued our discussion until about 2 a.m., the P.M. being continually interrupted by reports of what was happening in London. As we separated I asked Sir Charles if he was returning to Uxbridge that night. 'No,' he said, 'I am sleeping here. I don't suppose I shall ever have another chance of staying a night at Chequers.' Little did either of us know that he was then being vetted for the post of Chief of the Air Staff, the appointment in which he subsequently served with such distinction. As I turned in, I thought to myself: 'What a night! But the Prime Minister goes through something like this every night, cool, calm, and collected as always.'

Sir Winston, as we know, has a most inventive and imaginative mind, but he could not always be aware of the practical difficulties that would be met with in attempting to carry out some of his special schemes. He disliked being opposed and felt that difficulties were there 'to be overcome, not for the purpose of frustration', but when he was sure you were really trying to meet his wishes he would readily give way if you could produce sound arguments against them. In war, it frequently happens that material prepared for one purpose may suddenly be found invaluable for another and I think Sir Winston usually had this at the back of his mind when the continuance of any project was in doubt, especially if it concerned a quite new development of any kind. I can record two instances of his persistence. The first was early in the war when he wished to send the Fleet into the Baltic, together with the necessary supply ships. Naval opinion was strongly against the practicability of such an operation but Churchill said: 'Anyway, let us be ready.' For my part, it meant converting four of our best Clan Line merchant ships to carry five thousand tons of fuel and two thousand tons of ammunition. The instructions were that they must be completed in two months. This meant working night and day, and I knew that when the project was abandoned, as I felt certain it would be, the wasting of all this work would have the most adverse effect on our shipbuilders. The project was indeed abandoned, but as it turned out Admiral Cunningham, the C.-in-C. Mediterranean, found these ships to be exactly what he needed for the supply of Malta. Most naval people will remember the part played by the *Breconshire* until she was finally sunk off the southern corner of the island she had so gallantly helped to sustain.

The second instance concerns the time when we were very short of A.A. guns. Churchill persisted in the development of the A.A. rocket for ground-air defence, a scheme that was under the able direction of Sir Alwyn Crow. The consensus of expert opinion was that rockets were much too inaccurate for this purpose and we rather regretted the time and effort being spent on them. Our view turned out to be correct, but as time went on the rocket was found to be invaluable for many other purposes—such as rocket-assisted take-off, rocket-firing aircraft, and rocket-firing ships used for the support of landings. It was Churchill's foresight and persistence in supporting the work of Sir Alwyn that made all these things possible.

Sir Winston undertook many journeys in his own train with the object of seeing things for himself and I was among his party on four of these excursions—to Shoeburyness to see the development of an armour-piercing shell, to the South Coast to inspect the anti-invasion defences and watch the heavy naval guns being mounted, to the West Country to see the work being done on rocket development, and to Newcastle to try to accelerate progress on the *King George V* class battleships.

His energy amidst this variety of subjects, about each of which he knew as much as anyone, was amazing. After tramping through the mud and slush all day he would discuss the war and affairs of State far into the night with whatever distinguished visitors had been invited to meet him. On the journey to the West Country the P.M. decided to pay a visit *en route* to Swansea which had just suffered heavily from bombing. As he drove in a jeep through the shattered streets making the V-sign, the cheers of the people rang out all round him. Episodes such as this seemed to fortify the Prime Minister—not through any sense of personal pride, but rather through a renewed realization that the spirit of the people was as undaunted as his own.

One of the Prime Minister's important innovations

was the giving of a 'battle' name to each dangerous situation as it developed—for example, the Battle of Britain and the Battle of the Atlantic. A meeting was then convened every Wednesday morning at which all the Departments concerned were represented, usually by Ministers, and over which the Prime Minister presided. Nothing was discussed except 'The Battle' and the meetings were continued until it was won.

The 'Battle' I remember best was the Battle of the Atlantic. Among his various other duties Lord Cherwell, then Professor Lindemann, kept a record of all the statistics involved. At the start of the meeting he would produce the figures for the past week: submarines destroyed, merchant shipping sunk by the enemy, merchant tonnage building, merchant ships under repair, men employed on naval and merchant-ship work, the time taken to turn round ships in port, and so on. Then the Prime Minister would start questioning the Departments and, after discussion, decide upon whatever further action was required. If there seemed any shortcomings anywhere he never failed to put his finger on the right spot, so that one felt a little relieved when one's own Department was not the first to be tackled.

I recall two particular incidents that occurred at these weekly meetings. The first was at a time when the figures for merchant-ship sinkings were increasing alarmingly and the total tonnage of merchant ships under repair had risen to two million tons. Sir Winston asked the Admiralty, through whom all ship repairs were controlled (merchant ships being under Sir James Lithgow), to give definite priority to merchant-ship repairs over naval repairs for the time being. 'Not overriding priority,' he said, 'because that might stop all naval work and I don't believe in overriding priorities. Priority tempered with common sense.' The Admiralty agreed to this proposal and Sir James Lithgow and I took the appropriate action. About a fortnight later, when the figures came in to the Admiralty before the meeting, we saw that, although the tonnage of merchant vessels under repair had begun to grow less, the number of men employed, respectively, on merchant-ship and naval repairs remained about the same. Sir James said: 'Controller, I think we're for it this morning—but you worse than me!' 'I agree,' I answered, 'but the fact of the matter is that you can't take a naval ship with a large hole in her out of dock until she has been repaired, and this takes time. Besides, I don't believe the ship repairers always realize the effect of their labour statistics at the other end; it is so easy, when hard-pressed and having to fill up forms, to show the same figures as last week.' 'All the same,' said Sir James, 'you're for it.' Somewhat uneasily I walked over with him to the meeting. Sure enough, the Prime Minister came in looking like thunder, sat down, and looked at me. Sir James gave me a nudge. 'Controller,' said the Prime Minister, 'the manpower figures have not altered since I gave my instructions two weeks ago. You are deliberately disobeying my orders and obstinately holding on to your naval repairs.' A little taken aback, I was silent for a moment when Lord Beaverbrook (I think it was he) whispered to the P.M.: 'He's a mule.' I don't recollect whether Churchill nodded his head, but before he could speak again I said: 'Sir, you are being most unfair' and went on to put the case as I had done to Sir James Lithgow. Churchill said no more and went on to the next Department. I left the meeting a little perturbed at my audacity but I hadn't wanted the P.M. to think that I cared nothing for his instructions. A week later the statistics had improved, but I could not attend the Wednesday meeting on account of some emergency that required my attention elsewhere. In the afternoon the Prime Minister sent over to find out why he had not seen me at the meeting, and then I knew I had been forgiven. It was one of those kindly thoughts that endear Sir Winston to those who serve under him.

The other incident I remember demonstrates Sir Winston's attention to detail. The turn round time of ships in port had increased from eight days to thirteen. No one could quite say why. The only suggestion was that it must be due to the normal dislocation of war. 'If that is the case,' said Churchill, 'we must go into the details at the ports.' He appointed an admiral (Sir Henry Moore) with a small staff to go round every port in the country consulting with the port authorities as to whether any further action could be taken. And, indeed, to show how small things matter, in one of the smaller ports there were insufficient gangways to the ships for the men going aboard and coming ashore. It was not so much a lack of organization on the part of the port authority as the result of attempting, as everyone was doing at that time, to make do with what they had got.

In subsequent years I was far afield but, although I

was one among so many, the Prime Minister never failed to write and comment on any important appointment or event. And this was not a personal matter. It was most essential, and still is, that anyone serving in far distant waters should not be allowed to feel himself forgotten by the people at home. The Prime Minister always took the initiative in maintaining this close touch.

In recent months the Prime Minister said of me to a friend: 'The Admiral is a little difficult sometimes.' It would be highly impertinent of me to make any retort, but the fact remains that apart from what I have learned down the years from my own senior officers, I owe a very great deal to the training, the guidance, and the inspiration of Sir Winston Churchill.

Fraser of North Cape

Churchill
and the Commonwealth

by THE RT. HON. R. G. MÉNZIES

WHEN we consider the life of a great man, the real
task is to get behind or beyond the publicly recorded
facts, the facts of notoriety, and discover something of
the informal or unrecorded truth. When friends of
mine, full of inevitable eagerness to know something
of their (and my) hero, ask me what manner of man is
Winston Churchill, my first answer is: 'What a boy!'
and I am not sure that this is not my last answer also.
This should be explained, lest it be thought to be either
an impertinence or a purely conventional colloquialism.

Sir Winston Churchill has, marvellously mixed in
him, great elements. He has a masterly personality.
You have only to sit opposite him at a conference to
discover that. He has towering ability. He has tradition and background. He is not unaware, as his pen
has shown, of John Churchill, the first Duke of Marlborough and the greatest of English Commanders.
There is a family standard. It is not to be let down. It
is one of my own favourite themes that the sense of

continuity is the backbone of national and individual endurance. Compare the history of the early nineteenth-century Martello towers on the Kentish Coast, the crude weapons of the levies raised to meet a Napoleonic invasion, and the great speeches of the younger Pitt, with the barbed wire, the Home Guard, and the fire and the courage of the Churchill speeches 140 years later, and you will see what I mean. Great nations and great men do not spring suddenly from an infertile or unexpected soil. They are the product of centuries. The modern iconoclast, the clever but rootless pseudo-intellectual, scoffs at tradition. He is all for *a priori* reasoning and blueprints. He thinks men are made of paper and ink, and that at base they are a superior kind of calculating machine. Nothing could be more foolish. Certainly, nothing could be more un-English. For the English have never been academical and deductive. They have lived from problem to problem, solving each by boldness or compromise, moving almost always towards fairness and justice and good sense.

The history of England has been, therefore, a story of a tenacious and proud people, sometimes (and sometimes rightly) thought stodgy and unimaginative, a 'nation of shopkeepers', but throwing up, more than any other people on record, great statesmen and poets and thinkers as the sudden flowers of a land chilled by the snow, but warmed by the Gulf Stream. Shakespeare, Hampden, Cromwell, Milton, Marlborough, Chatham, Pitt, Disraeli, Lloyd George, Churchill are, properly considered, no accidental phenomena. They are the recurring product of a rich national tradition. In brief, Churchill is the Englishman *par excellence*, full of perfection and imperfection, at all times human and understandable, yet rising to great issues with an almost divine power and character and authority.

How does such a man come to be the acknowledged leader of a great Commonwealth of Nations? Not by a process of conscious reason, for the people of Britain did not achieve an Empire or a Commonwealth consciously. Indeed, for those born and bred in the great British tradition, there is historic interest in the accidental nature of the Empire, but some modern irritation in the casual outlook upon that Empire of some men of standing and influence in the Old Land. It is the fashion of the modern Communist, modern in his destructive thinking, but medieval in his sense of human values, to speak of British (or American) 'Imperialism'. To listen to him and believe him would be to accept the idea that our race went out consciously to conquer the world, and that every movement from colonialism to self-government has been involuntary and reluctant. What are the facts? We achieved America by enterprise, sometimes viewed suspiciously at Westminster, and lost it by a mixture of want of imagination, misunderstanding, and military incompetence. We established Australia, not because we saw a great new British world, for indeed the very outlines of Australia were dim in the Southern Seas, but because the American Revolution had made it necessary to found a new penal settlement which could accommodate a small fraction of those who could, and did, violate the inhuman and sometimes quite pedantic criminal laws of 150 years ago. The great founders of Empire, famous now, were in their day treated as odd and embarrassing fellows who were creating liabilities and not assets. Warren Hastings was impeached, the scandal of the impeachment modified for us only by the eloquence of Edmund Burke. The founder of British power in Aden was discarded and disgraced. The great Governor of Singapore gave his name to a gentleman burglar of modern English fiction. And, long before that, Walter Raleigh had secured no merit from exploration, except that of a brave death.

Why, then, in the last hundred years, have we become familiar with, and proud of, an Empire and a Commonwealth? Part of the answer is, of course, that achievement brings pride. But the other part of the answer is that, as a race, we have a faculty for 'making the best of it', for 'making it work'. And so we have become partners and actors in a modern Empire which is not Imperialist, which has got rid of tyranny, which, like tall mountain trees, has grown ever towards the light, and which has, in the result, proved to be the greatest essay in united democracy, the greatest reconciliation of independence and inter-dependence, of monarchy and self-government, that the world has ever seen.

Those considerations bring me back to Winston Spencer Churchill. He is not a Joseph Chamberlain. He has not been particularly identified with great Empire economic policies. He is much too European for that. No man can serve two masters. He can hardly hope to devote his thought and power to European balance, to the affairs of that old world which has produced most of the conflicts for the new, and at the same time stand in spirit among the factories of Australia or the green farms of New Zealand, or breathe 'the spicy breezes that blow o'er Ceylon's Isle'.

If this seems critical, put it down to the proverb-attested truth that a cat may look at a king. For the great glory of our present generation is that a great Englishman, wearing his Empire with a difference, was raised up by God to be, in the greatest crisis of our history, not only the great Empire man, but the trusted champion of British freedom, so soon and so dramatically to be seen as the freedom of the world.

Winston Churchill had for many years been a controversial figure in Australia. Not known in person, he was in turn thought of as brilliant, unstable, brave, indiscreet, born to be a minority leader. So recently as in 1939, he was, so it was said, a spent force. And then, in 1940, as the Great War reached its sudden and terrible climax, he emerged, not only as the resolute and flaming leader of his own people, but as the unquestioned leader of the entire British world. On thousands of Australian farms, in factory and counting-house throughout a dozen nations, he became, almost overnight, the man of destiny and the familiar friend, the voice of courage and defiance, the common spokesman and inspirer of the British people, clear across the world.

To repeat such statements is to be platitudinous. I will therefore not repeat them. But there is a lesson to be learned, and I will content myself by stating it, as I understand it.

For too many years men, learned and otherwise, had occupied their time in considering somewhat legalistically the structure and mechanics of the Empire.

These were important, but much more important was the spirit, the sense of comradeship, the high surge of the human pulse. The great Imperialists in half a dozen countries had made millions think the Empire; it was left to Winston, the Englishman and European, to make scores of millions feel it with passion and will.

It is one of the blessed oddities of the human memory that we remember good and happy things rather more readily than miseries and despairs. It is well, therefore, to recall that during the Second World War there were moments and months of acute danger and anxiety, and that when France fell in 1940, and until Hitler's invasion of Russia more than a year later, the greatest burden of the war was carried by Great Britain and the fighting Commonwealth. And what a burden it was. The heroic disasters of Dunkirk and Calais; the subsequent improvisation of men and of material; the Battle of Britain; the vast and almost unsung Battle of the Atlantic; the British Commonwealth struggle in the Mediterranean and the Middle East; these crises of the war were surmounted against all odds and, indeed, against all probabilities. They could not have been achieved without sublime leadership, fired by courage and patriotism, appealing not only to the mind but to the heart and enduring tenacity of a great people. What is the secret of this immense power? The question is unanswerable, for genius does not explain itself, and we who do not possess genius do badly to try to analyse it.

But some things can, and should be said. They are inadequate, but they are true.

First of all, Winston Churchill has faith in himself.

This superb quality, not to be confused with conceit, sustained him through years in which many people did not believe in him at all. Conceit is a shallow and foolish thing, commonly one facet of an ignorant but pretentious mind. But Winston's self-confidence is one facet of a courageous and richly-furnished mind. It is, in truth, an expression of his double courage; a physical courage well-attested at Omdurman and in South Africa; a moral courage which took him through years of political unpopularity to the greatest heights of acclaim reached by mortal man in the twentieth century.

Second, he knows his own people. In the war he spoke, not as a gifted stranger, but in the accents of the English, with the deep brool of the British lion in his voice. With that homely but arresting simplicity of speech which only the greatest masters of England can attain, he was understood by all, and so was able to inspire all. This remarkable quality of clear and colloquial eloquence can all too easily be underestimated by those who distrust words and who, with grievous error, distrust fine speech, as if it were something independent of fine thought. Great leaders must have great ideas and great force of character. But if ideas and character are to be made to move to action and to endurance they must, in a nation or group of nations in which blind and illiterate obedience to authority is rapidly passing away, be allied to a rare power of exposition and advocacy. It was indeed a happy stroke of fate that against the sheer ranting mob-mastery of Hitler and Mussolini, raving to millions of people who had, for the nonce, sold themselves into intellectual and moral slavery, there should be set a Churchill who

could, and did, with richer power of speech, raise his
people, touch their spirits to noble issues, and give to
every individual a new sense of power and responsibility.

Third, he has that most precious of commodities, a
rich and chuckling and sometimes impish sense of
humour. I once ventured to say that the conflict between totalitarian and democratic countries was, at
bottom, a conflict between those who could not laugh,
and those who could. This is, of course, an over-
simplification. But I would be prepared to assert that
the rich humour of the British people, under blitz and
privation and misery, was the conclusive weapon of the
war. Laughter is of the essence of democracy; it cannot
be taught, and it cannot be commanded. It is an individual thing, an intricate thing. Winston Churchill's
chuckle, coming to the free people of the world over a
million radios, was an unbelievable stimulant to plain
men and women, who chuckled in their turn, and so
grew in sanity and strength.

Fourth, in the homely phrase, he loved and loves
his job.

He stood boldly in the breach, and rejoiced to be
alive. In the course of a long political life, I have seen
and known men in whom the pride and pleasure of
office had obscured the sense of a duty which is often
drudgery. Others have gone to the other extreme,
and have done their work as if they were blind to all
else. But Churchill is like no others. He toiled and
sweated in his leadership; his labours were versatile
and tremendous; his sense of responsibility in the long
and bitter agonies of the war was massive and un-

remitting. Yet in a real and human sense, he enjoyed it all. He got his own fun out of his own misery; he relished difficulties, because it was a pleasure to overcome them; he went on working day after day, night after night, because work was wonderful!

I well remember, in about March of 1941, being at a War Cabinet meeting at Downing Street when a proposal was advanced for giving a few weeks' holiday leave, on some sort of roster, to senior civil servants who had been carrying grievous and continuous burdens. It seemed to us at the table to be an eminently reasonable and, indeed, essential proposal. It no doubt seemed right to Winston; but he came out instantly with the perfect expression of what I have just been trying to explain about him. 'Well,' he said, 'I suppose, since you insist, that I must agree. But I confess that I do not understand how anybody, privileged before history to play a part in this mighty struggle, can bear to be separated from his duty for even five minutes!'

In this short analysis I have said nothing about the obvious; Churchill's vast intellectual grasp, his habit of command, his profound knowledge of the history and mechanism of war, his devotion to his country. I have rather sought to discover those subtle and human elements which enabled him to turn defeat into victory, and which made him, in great areas of the British Commonwealth which he had never seen, a pillar of fire by night and of cloud by day.

Robert Menzies

The Master of Words

by A. P. HERBERT

THE word 'oratory', says the *Pocket Oxford Dictionary*, means 'rhetoric, speeches, eloquent language, highly-coloured presentment of facts'. 'The conditions of modern life,' says the *Encyclopædia Britannica*, 'and especially the invention of printing, have to some extent diminished the importance which belonged in antiquity to the art of speaking, though modern democratic politics and forensic conditions still make it one which may be cultivated with advantage.' If either of these learned authorities had heard any of Sir Winston Churchill's war-time speeches they must have chosen other words. Oratory, surely, is speech in action (excluding, of course, the sergeant-majors and policemen). Millions of men can 'make a speech' which does no more harm than a passing fly—and leaves no more behind it. The 'orator' is a person of power. He may appeal to the sense of logic (as Aristotle, rather foolishly, insisted that he must), to the sense of justice, or duty, the sublime or the ridiculous. But, one way or another, he stirs the hearts and minds of men as he desires, commanding their deeds or endurance, their judgment or their money, their verdict or their votes. There must, of course, be something more than words—character, 'personality', delivery—and occasion. The wrong man can make the finest phrase ineffective. If certain statesmen I have heard had uttered the famous speech of King Henry V not a man would have felt like moving into the breach. Long ago I wrote (intending no malice towards Mr. Neville Chamberlain, whom I admired more than many did): 'That was one great difference between Mr. Churchill and Mr. Chamberlain. He after all, was tough enough, and since the war began, had been heart and soul with Mr. Churchill. But when he said the fine true thing it was like a faint air played on a pipe and lost on the wind at once. When Mr. Churchill said it, it was like an organ filling the church, and we all went out refreshed and resolute to do or die.'

By any standard, by any definition, he is a great orator. Mr. Lloyd George, I thought, in my early days in the House, gave a better 'performance', in the theatrical sense—richer in histrionic gesture, sudden whispers, and changes of key. Mr. Bevan at his best, perhaps, has more of the actor's arts, which, in this affair, are not to be despised. But Churchill, to say nothing of character and all that, is the supreme master of language. He has always the right words for every occasion, whether he makes demands of our manhood or our mirth: and the wonder is how often he is able to find a new way of saying an old or ordinary thing. The words need not be new; they are not long Latin words, they cannot always be classed as 'highly-coloured':

most often they are short and simple words with which
we have all been long familiar; but by some magic of
his own he can put them together like a bunch of wild
flowers so that something new and beautiful is made.
Of the late Queen Mary he said in the House of Commons: 'She looked a Queen: she acted like a Queen.'
How simple—how 'obvious', once it is said! But no
one else thought of packing so much treasure in so
small a casket.

How many of the most famous words, the electric
words of Hitler's War, were short words, words of
one syllable! I was fortunate to hear most of them in
the House of Commons, the words that passed into
history, and literature, as soon as they were spoken:
and nothing I have heard on any stage has been more
moving. Take the famous speech of 13 May 1940,
after his appointment as Prime Minister. Hitler had
Norway and was roaring to the Channel. Poor France
was rolling down the hill. We were likely to be left
alone, as we had not been for centuries, with a powerful
enemy at Calais and Cherbourg. But there at the table,
there at the despatch box, where Sir Edward Grey, in
1914, had said: 'The lights are going out over Europe,'
stood this one man, with the pale, round, bull-dog face,
grim but undaunted, ready to lead us, 'if necessary, alone'.

I would say to the House, as I have said to those
who have joined this Government: 'I have nothing
to offer but blood, toil, tears, and sweat.'

We have before us an ordeal of the most grievous
kind. We have before us many, many long months
of struggle and of suffering. You ask what is our

policy? I will say: It is to wage war, by sea, land, and air, with all our might and with all the strength that God can give us: to wage war against a monstrous tyranny, never surpassed in the dark, lamentable catalogue of human crime. That is our policy. You ask, What is our aim? I can answer in one word: Victory—victory at all costs, victory in spite of all terror, victory, however long and hard the road may be; for without victory, there is no survival. Let that be realized; no survival for the British Empire; no survival for all that the British Empire has stood for, no survival for the urge and impulse of the ages, that mankind will move forward towards its goal. But I take up my task with buoyancy and hope. I feel sure that our cause will not be suffered to fail among men. At this time I feel entitled to claim the aid of all, and I say, 'Come, then, let us go forward together with our united strength.'

All the world has quoted the historic four one-syllable words of that speech, and no one has dared to parody or adapt them for the baser purposes of after-dinner speaking. But two years later, in the Vote of Censure Debate of 1 July 1942, Churchill himself referred to them, in singular but characteristic fashion:

I have not made any arrogant, confident, boasting predictions at all. On the contrary, I have stuck hard to my blood, toil, tears, and sweat, to which I have added muddle and mismanagement, and that, to some extent, I must admit, is what you have got out of it.

Then there was that tremendous assembly of short explosive words in the speech that followed Dunkirk (4 June 1940):

I have, myself, full confidence that if all do their duty, if nothing is neglected, and the best arrangements are made, as they are being made, we shall prove ourselves once again able to defend our island home, to ride out the storm of war, and to outlive the menace of tyranny, if necessary for years, if necessary alone. At any rate, that is what we are going to try to do. That is the resolve of His Majesty's Government—every man of them. That is the will of Parliament and the nation. The British Empire and the French Republic linked together in their cause and need, will defend to the death their native soil, aiding each other like good comrades to the utmost of their strength. Even though large tracts of Europe and many old and famous States have fallen or may fall into the grip of the Gestapo and all the odious apparatus of Nazi rule, we shall not flag or fail. We shall go on to the end, we shall fight in France, we shall fight on the seas and oceans, we shall fight with growing confidence and growing strength in the air, we shall defend our island, whatever the cost may be, we shall fight on the beaches, we shall fight on the landing grounds, we shall fight in the fields and in the streets, we shall fight in the hills; we shall never surrender, and even if, which I do not for a moment believe, this island or a large part of it were subjugated and starving, then our Empire beyond the seas, armed and guarded by the British Fleet, would carry on the struggle, until, in God's good time, the new world, with all its power and might, steps forth to the rescue and the liberation of the old.

Any man might have said, many would have said: 'Our policy is to continue the struggle; all our forces and resources will be mobilized: and we have every hope of ultimate success.' That might have been enough: for neither Parliament nor people proposed to give in. But most of us were thinking, none the less, 'How on earth are we going to do it? and what happens next? What happens, especially, if France falls, as Mr. Churchill clearly fears?' The greatness of that speech was that it filled in, with simple, vivid strokes, a picture of the impossible made possible. Every man saw himself in that picture somewhere, fighting 'on the beaches, in the streets, in the hills': and we all went out refreshed and resolute to do our best. If Churchill saw a way out of this mess—even if the worst happened and Britain fell as well—that was good enough for us. The details we were willing to leave to him. He himself, I believe, has modestly said that in that speech, and others, he was merely expressing what was in the minds of the people. I think there was rather more to it than that. The trumpet does not sound for nothing.

Thirteen days later he has to speak to the people 'on the air' about the collapse of France. See how he begins—and ends:

'The news from France is very bad.' (It is in my mind that he began one speech in the House of Commons with these blunt words: 'The war is not going well.' I cannot find them, and may have imagined them: but he is never afraid, as other statesmen are, of a prompt plunge into the depths of the matter.)

The news from France is very bad and I grieve for the gallant French people who have fallen into this terrible misfortune. Nothing will alter our feelings towards them or our faith that the genius of France will rise again. What has happened in France makes no difference to our actions and purpose. We have become the sole champions now in arms to defend the world cause. We shall do our best to be worthy of this high honour. We shall defend our island home and with the British Empire we shall fight on unconquerable until the curse of Hitler is lifted from the brows of mankind. We are sure that in the end all will come right.

Always the same message: 'Do your best—all will be well.' But he had to say it over and over again, and in what a multitude of modes he contrived to say it! How glad I shall always be that I heard with my own ears the 'Finest Hour' oration on 18 June 1940. On that day Hitler and Mussolini met at Munich to decide the terms to be imposed on fallen France. He began by relating briefly the failure of the High Command in France, but he went on:

I am not reciting these facts for the purpose of recrimination. That I judge to be utterly futile and even harmful. We cannot afford it. I recite them to explain why it was that we did not have, as we could have had, between twelve and fourteen British divisions in the line in this great battle, instead of only three. Now I put all this aside. I put it on the shelf, from which the historians, when they have time, will select their documents to tell their stories. We have to think of the future and not of the past. This also applies in a small way to our own affairs at home.

See now with what magnanimity and wisdom the greatest critic of 'Munich', without mentioning the word, dismissed the very thought from all men's minds as he had thrust it from his own, with Mr. Neville Chamberlain behind him:

There are many who would hold an inquest in the House of Commons on the conduct of the Governments—and of Parliaments, for they are in it too—during the years which led up to this catastrophe. They seek to indict those who were responsible for the guidance of our affairs. This also would be a foolish and pernicious process. There are too many in it. Let each man search his conscience and search his speeches. I frequently search mine.

Of this I am quite sure, that if we open a quarrel between the past and the present, we shall find that we have lost the future. Therefore, I cannot accept the drawing of any distinctions between Members of the present Government. . . .

'Do your best.' In what new way could you or I have said it that day? He discovered two. One, very simple and understanding, for the ordinary citizen, soon to be confronted with ordeal by bombing:

I do not at all underrate the severity of the ordeal which lies before us: but I believe our countrymen will show themselves capable of standing up to it, like the brave men of Barcelona, and will be able to stand up to it, and carry on in spite of it, at least as well as any other people in the world. Much will depend upon this; every man and every woman will have the chance to show the finest qualities of their race, and render the highest service to their cause. For all of us, at this time, whatever our sphere, our station, our occupation or our duties, it will be a help to remember the famous lines:

'He nothing common did or mean
Upon that memorable scene.'

By this time, we knew in the House of Commons that however fine the earlier movements of the symphony had been it would end with some surpassing procession of chords that would stir the soul of a sheep. We looked forward to those endings with excitement, and this was one of the finest, the most powerfully delivered, of all:

What General Weygand called the Battle of France is over. I expect that the Battle of Britain is about to begin. Upon this battle depends the survival of Christian civilization. Upon it depends our own British life, and the long continuity of our institutions and our Empire. The whole fury and might of the enemy must very soon be turned on us. Hitler knows that he will have to break us in this island or lose the war. If we can stand up to him, all Europe may be free and the life of the world may move forward into broad sunlit uplands. But if we fail, then the whole world, including the United States, including all that we have known and cared for, will sink into the abyss of a new dark age made more sinister, and perhaps more protracted, by the lights of perverted science. Let us therefore brace ourselves to our duties, and so bear ourselves that, if the British Empire and its Commonwealth last for a thousand years, men will still say: 'This was their finest hour.'

Read this, or any other passage, aloud, and mark how easily it runs. The pauses make themselves. They say that the first draft of the speech is done by dictation, and gets its speaking, as opposed to literary, quality in this way. I do not know.

The main mystery is how such speeches, at such a time, were ever prepared at all. The fine, famous sayings (note again, by the way, all these words of one syllable)—'Their finest hour'—'Never in the field of human conflict was so much owed by so many to so few' —'Give us the tools, and we will finish the job'—may seem obvious, like fine tunes, once they are heard: but they were not obvious before. The mine is rich, no doubt, and some of the jewels may have been found near the surface: but many others had to be dug for, polished and elegantly set. And this orator was not free to sit in a study all day, at work upon his gems: he was busy day and night at the innumerable details and duties of running a war and managing a Government.

One of my favourite 'endings' did not, I think, attract so much public attention as some of the others at the time. On 7 May 1941 a Vote of Confidence in the Government was carried by 447 votes to 3. At the end of a long, detailed speech about military affairs the Prime Minister said:

It is a year almost to a day since, in the crash of the disastrous Battle of France, His Majesty's present Administration was formed. Men of all parties, duly authorized by their parties, joined hands together to fight this business to the end.

(Observe—'joined hands together'—not 'agreed to co-operate' or 'consented to a Coalition'.)

That was a dark hour, and little did we know what storms and perils lay before us, and little did Herr Hitler know, when in June 1940 he received the total capitulation of France and when he expected to be master of all Europe in a few weeks and the world in a few years, that ten months later, in May 1941, he would be appealing to the much-tried German people to prepare themselves for the war of 1942. When I look back on the perils which have been overcome, upon the great mountain waves through which the gallant ship has driven, when I remember all that has gone wrong, and remember also all that has gone

right, I feel sure we have no need to fear the
tempest. Let it roar, and let it rage. We shall come
through.

'Let it roar——' The words are one-syllablers again,
the metaphor is old and simple: but I remember what a
trumpet-call it was. Those were the last words he spoke
in the old Chamber: for three days later the Germans
brilliantly replied to that defiance by destroying the
House of Commons. But they laughed too soon. We
did 'come through'.

But, it may be said, all these were high dramatic
occasions making it easy for a man of such powers to
utter something memorable. But that is to forget all the
long, laborious marshalling of facts and arguments
that went before. Few will remember the many speeches
of the years before the war on such dull subjects as the
Minister of Supply, where the orator had no present
peril, no common emotion, to help him, only the per-
suasive power of facts and figures and faith: but they
were such solid and worthy work as all must envy, and
the young should study.

Consider, too, the grim and gallant speech of 2 July
1942, when he was facing enemies at home, now, as
well as those abroad. On 1 July we began the discussion
of a Vote of Censure: '*That this House . . . has no confidence in the central direction of the war.*' It was supported by powerful, patriotic men of all parties, men
who had clamoured for him in 1940. It was, in the
minds of many, and the mouths of some, a 'Churchill
Must Go' movement. It was by forces no stronger than
these that Mr. Neville Chamberlain had been cast

down: and Chamberlain then had only one defeat to his account—Churchill had a dozen. He may well have thought: After all that I have done—is this the beginning of the end? As if all this were not enough, Rommel chose that very day to open his assault on the gates of Alexandria. All through the two days of tense debate, while listening to the 'diatribes' of Mr. Bevan and others, he found it difficult, as he said, 'to withdraw my thoughts from the tremendous and most critical battle now raging in Egypt'. What was happening there, at the door to the Suez Canal? Those two days may well have been among the worst of the war, for the man in charge: and that speech, accordingly, I reckon among the best.

With his first words he proclaimed the right of all-comers to bait and attack him:

This long Debate has now reached its final stage. What a remarkable example it has been of the un-bridled freedom of our Parliamentary institutions in times of war! Everything that could be thought of or raked up has been used to weaken confidence in the Government. . . . All this poured out by cable and radio to all parts of the world, to the distress of all our friends and to the delight of all our foes. I am in favour of this freedom, which no other country would use, or dare to use, in times of mortal peril such as those through which we are passing. But the story must not end there, and I make now my appeal to the House of Commons to make sure that it does not end there.

Then he spoke for ninety minutes—twenty-six columns of Hansard.

They included a happy example of the wit and humour that are so formidable a part of his armoury. About half-way through he was asked, by Mr. Hore-Belisha:

'What about the Churchill tank?'

'This tank,' said the prisoner at the bar, 'the A.22, was ordered off the drawing-board, and large numbers went into production quickly. As might be expected, it had many defects and teething troubles, and when these became apparent it was appropriately rechristened the "Churchill".' (There was a general, and sympathetic, chuckle at that.) 'These defects have now been largely overcome. I am sure that this tank will prove, in the end, a powerful, massive, and serviceable weapon of war.'

It does not look much on paper, perhaps, for those who were not present at the grim, dramatic scene. But I remember how we laughed that day. The little joke, perfectly timed, turned against himself, and yet obliquely an answer to all that had been said, eased the tension everywhere and made all men one for a moment. Some said that it turned the whole course of the debate. That may be too much to say; for, after all, twenty-five Members still voted against him. But it gave us all a lesson in how to 'mix the bowling'. Nearly always, in the most solemn speeches, there was some sudden quip that made the whole House happy.

He brought those two black days to an end with the strength of Ulysses bending his great bow:

I do not know what my critics would like me to say now. If I predict success and speak in buoyant terms and misfortune continues, their tongues and pens will be able to dilate on my words. On the other hand, if I predict failure and paint the picture in the darkest hues—I have painted it in pretty dark hues—I might safeguard myself against one danger, but only at the expense of a struggling Army. Also I might be wrong. So I will say nothing about the future except to invite the House and the nation to face with courage whatever it may unfold. . . .

The setting down of this Vote of Censure by Members of all parties is a considerable event. Do not, I beg you, let the House underrate the gravity of what has been done. It has been trumpeted all round the world to our disparagement, and when every nation, friend and foe, is waiting to see what is the true resolve and conviction of the House of Commons, it must go forward to the end. All over the world, throughout the United States, as I can testify, in Russia, far away in China and throughout every subjugated country all our friends are waiting to know whether there is a strong, solid Government in Britain and whether its national leadership is to be challenged or not. Every vote counts. If those who have assailed us are reduced to contemptible proportions and their Vote of Censure on the National Government is converted to a vote of censure upon its authors, make no mistake, a cheer will go up from every friend of Britain and every faithful servant of our cause, and the knell of disappointment will ring in the ears of the tyrants we are striving to over-throw.'

The House divided: Ayes 25; Noes, 475.

I am glad that I was one of the 475. Three months later, the Battle of El Alamein was fought. There were no more votes of no confidence. The orator had won his Alamein on the 2nd of July.

A. P. Herbert.

The Chronicler

by Sir Charles Webster

'To do justice to a great man,' wrote Sir Winston Churchill long ago, 'discriminating criticism is necessary. Gush, however quenching, is always insipid.'[1] It is always wise to follow the advice of Sir Winston in such matters, but, if that course be attempted in this paper, it is necessary to begin with the fundamental fact. No other eminent man of action has ever given to the world so splendid an account of the age in which he lived as Sir Winston Churchill has done. This superiority is of course partly due to the greatness of his achievements. He has written of great events of which he could often say *quorum pars magna fui.* Other great figures have essayed a similar task; none has accomplished it with the same success. Julius Cæsar, the most famous of all chroniclers, gave after all only a dry summary of events. In more modern times Frederick the Great stands out from all others in the quantity and

(NOTE: Acknowledgement is made to the B.B.C. and the *Spectator* for permission to reprint in this chapter certain passages from the author's broadcast review of *The Second World War*, Vol. I, and from his review in the *Spectator* of Vol. II.)

[1] *The River War*, Vol. II, p. 375.

quality of his writings, but he was not a master of the language which he used. Napoleon had not sufficient patience to write himself, and devoted his exile to constructing a legend through the medium of others. Metternich's account of the earlier part of his political career shows characteristic vanity and obscurity. Talleyrand's *Mémoires*, though they have had an amazing success in deceiving posterity, mainly depended on a collection of letters, many of which he did not write himself. French history of the nineteenth century has, indeed, been adorned by a profusion of memoirs. But of these only that of Guizot can in any way rank in importance with the work of Churchill, and though it is elaborately documented and written with the skill of a trained historian, it is inferior in candour and often deals in trivialities. Thiers, who had a greater power of compelling narrative, devoted his talents to the history of the preceding epoch. The greatest figure in Germany tried his hand, but the *Reflections and Reminiscences* of Bismarck, though they contain some pregnant passages, were so loose and inchoate as to be the despair of those who assisted him.

It is, moreover, only in our own generation that such chronicles have been given to the world immediately after the events which they describe. A new and voracious public awaits them. Proprietors of great journals compete for them before they are put between boards. They can be distributed all over the world and fortunes can be made out of them larger than those once won by a lifetime in the Indies. President Eisenhower revealed in the course of the last election that he had obtained such a one by means of a single volume. The supply of such chronicles has naturally grown with the demand, and many statesmen, and diplomats, soldiers, sailors, and airmen, have attempted at the same time to fortify their reputations against criticism and their declining years against the ravages of inflation.

But none of these modern chronicles can compare in breadth of outlook, majesty of style, wealth of documentation, courage, candour, and knowledge of past history, with the twelve volumes in which Sir Winston has described his own part in two world wars. Of our own Prime Ministers, Lord Balfour and Lord Asquith postponed the task until too late, and the one could only manage to produce a fragment, and the other failed to complete a rather dull survey. Lloyd George was, indeed, given a long interval of leisure in which he plied a diligent pen, but his works, though they contained many secret and important documents and had a ready sale, revealed that he possessed none of the qualities of a great writer. In the United States men of action often found it necessary to employ some other hand to translate their reminiscences into readable prose. Both in this country and the United States a minor figure has occasionally produced a book which can be read with pleasure as well as with profit, but for the most part their works show too obviously the motives that brought them into existence. In France the standard of writing is far higher. But one chronicle alone, that of Poincaré, seems to me to bear comparison with Churchill's and the Frenchman is obviously inferior in the range of his activities and the comprehension of what he had accomplished. In all countries, some in seeking to justify themselves have injured no one's reputation more than their own. The prime example, I suppose, is Prince Bülow, whose four volumes revealed how much a man could write himself down.

Churchill has not only escaped these dangers but added fresh lustre to his name, and in a short essay on so large a theme, it is, perhaps, more rewarding to dwell on the reasons for his success than on the writings themselves which all know and cherish. Like most good things it is due to a combination of character, training, and opportunity. Churchill became a good chronicler by the hard way, by practice and study. Necessity and inclination led him to become a journalist as well as a soldier when still a very young man and he thus acquired, no doubt, part of the fluency and clarity of his style. But he would not have developed his other qualities had he not at the same time undertaken to educate himself after his schools had failed so completely to understand the most brilliant of all their scholars. He has himself described in one of the most delightful of his books how the young subaltern in the long and torrid interval between drill in the early morning and polo in the late afternoon devoted himself to the study of great literature including the great English historians. The two greatest, Gibbon and Macaulay, left a permanent impression on his style and method of work. From Gibbon he derived the balanced and ironical apophthegms which appear at intervals in his works, so that Churchill profited at one remove from the dead languages which he had failed to appreciate while a schoolboy. This influence can be easily seen in the remarkable book, the second of his chronicles, which he wrote at the age of twenty-five, *The River War*. Here is a typical sentence: 'The simplicity of the instruction was aided by the zeal of the students, and learning grew beneath the palm trees more quickly perhaps than in the more magnificent schools of civilization.'[1] Occasionally the young author fell with a crash as when he used such a phrase as 'the malodorous incense of civilisation was offered to the startled gods of Egypt',[2] to describe the smoke of a railway engine. But nearly always these sonorous sentences add to the effect already produced on the reader by the gravity and sense of responsibility shown in the narrative. This influence is still apparent though it has been refined into the simpler style which Sir Winston has acquired by long practice.

But the fact that *The River War* remains more than fifty years later an indispensable guide to a great episode in imperial history was due to qualities which do not derive from Gibbon. It was Macaulay that Churchill made his model in the art of constructing a book. He has told us how he gradually became aware of the important relations between sentences, paragraphs, and chapters, how the paragraphs must fit together 'like the automatic couplings of railway carriages', how each chapter 'should be of equal value and more or less of equal length', how hard it is to weave into an 'integral theme' a number of diverse incidents, and how 'the work must be surveyed as a whole and due proportion and strict order be observed from beginning to end'. 'I already knew,' he adds, 'that chronology is the key to easy narrative. I already realized that "good sense is the foundation of good writing."'[3] All this seems a little

[1] *The River War*, Vol. I, pp. 280–1.
[2] Ibid. Vol. I, p. 290.
[3] *My Early Life*, pp. 225–6.

naïve to the sophisticated reader until he realizes that, as so often, Churchill was digging down to fundamentals which he intended should be the guide of future conduct.

But of course the lucid narrative style, lit up at regular intervals by an arresting metaphor or a sudden thrust of irony or humour, could not have been obtained by following a set of rules, however soundly based. It is practice that makes perfect. Churchill began as a war correspondent, a career which he was able to combine with that of a subaltern in a cavalry regiment. If occasionally the dual role caused him some embarrassment, it gave him the opportunity not only of observing but taking part in the events which he described. His obvious capacity, as well as a pertinacity which sometimes tried the patience of his superiors, enabled him nearly always to be at hand when affairs became exciting. He penetrated also into circles where subalterns are not generally given much scope and from the first was as much interested in strategy and administration as in tactics and picturesque incident. At the same time he was as eager for action as any of his fellows and was thus able to describe the fighting with inside knowledge. No doubt his birth and connections helped to secure him his opportunities. But, once the chance was obtained, he showed himself the equal of more professional rivals and was eagerly read by a select public.

These despatches were the foundation of the chronicles which rapidly followed them when the fighting was over, and it is amazing how quickly they were turned into books, which took account of the history and geography of the theatre of operations, and contained many reflections on the strategy and tactics of the campaigns and did justice to the point of view of the enemy, whether Pathan, Dervish, or Boer.

In this way Churchill described frontier fighting in India in *The Story of the Malakand Field Force* and the Sudan expedition in the two volumes of *The River War*. His two books on the South African War were less carefully prepared and *From London to Ladysmith via Pretoria* and *Ian Hamilton's March* merely transcribe his despatches with some corrections and amendments. The South African War remained a subject for lectures by which Churchill helped to finance himself during the period before the First World War.

And here, be it remembered that Churchill is not only a chronicler of contemporary events but also a successful biographer and historian. His life of his father has been held by some to be the best biography of a nineteenth-century statesman, while his *Life of Marlborough* has been treated with respect and admiration by experts in the same field even if they have not always agreed with its conclusions. These two works belong to a different category of writing, and must be judged by other standards and are outside the scope of this paper. But in producing them Churchill learnt much that enabled him to excel in contemporary history just as his skill as a chronicler assisted him as a historian.

But all this preparation and practice in the art of writing does not account for the whole of Churchill's success. He is an artist. It is for others to say how far he is successful on canvas, but he can certainly put on paper what he sees and feels. He has great powers of observation, and decisive, violent, or rapid action forms indelible pictures in his mind. To see the picture, however, is one thing; to describe it and the emotions it arouses in the observer is another. Churchill has always been able to communicate to others something of the excitement, pity, horror, and admiration which is produced in him by the contemplation of the tempestuous times in which he has lived.

Thus, though practice and constant endeavour have increased his powers, he was, in fact, born a chronicler. At any rate in *The River War* he shows many of the characteristics of his later writings. The historical introduction which forms the first part of the book no doubt owes much to information derived from the officials and soldiers whom he met during the campaign, but it is solidly based on documentary evidence distilled into a coherent and lucid narrative. He also exhibits an understanding both of the Egyptian and Sudanese soldiers and of the Dervish enemy, showing a magnanimity rare in any case and amazingly so in a young subaltern who had just taken part in the famous charge of the 21st Lancers at the battle of Omdurman. Not only the Mahdi, but an even more debatable figure, his successor, the Khalifa, are treated with discernment and even with sympathy. Some of his sternest judgments, indeed, are reserved for those directing the policy of his own country, including the most famous figure of them all, his commander-in-chief, Sir Herbert Kitchener, who had just been acclaimed in London as one of the greatest of our soldiers and appointed Governor-General of the Sudan.

For one of the principal characteristics of Churchill's writings is the courage and candour with which he has always stated his opinion of his contemporaries. These are so clearly inspired by impersonal motives that the charge of malice, pique, or jealousy has, I think, never been made. It certainly could not be sustained for a moment. For this reason it must have been sometimes all the more difficult for men to endure these magisterial pronouncements on their good and bad qualities couched in such compelling and incisive language. In this case, though Sir Herbert Kitchener was given full measure of praise as a great strategist and capable administrator, much else that he had done had failed to please his young critic, who had combined the dual position of a subaltern in his victorious army and correspondent o the *Morning Post*. The Sirdar's tactics were faulty and caused unnecessary loss of life, his demeanour so cold as to be almost inhuman. 'The Sirdar,' wrote Churchill, 'looked only to the soldiers who could march and fight. The wounded Egyptians, and latterly the wounded British soldier, did not excite his interest, and of all the departments of his army the one neglected was that concerned with the care of the sick and injured.'[1] It must have been hard for any commander to read words like these, though no doubt they were fully justified. It is hardly surprising that when Churchill returned to South Africa to continue his career as a war correspondent in the Boer War, he found that the three most important generals, Roberts, Kitchener, and French were by no means pleased with his reappearance on the scene of their activities. Yet all three became his firm friends, Lord Roberts almost immediately, and Lord Kitchener and Sir John French in later years.

In his later works Churchill has continued to make

[1] *The River War*, Vol. II, p. 377.

these considered judgments of his contemporaries though they have somewhat mellowed with the passing of years. And it must be remembered that his praise is just as forthright as his censure. It is bestowed especially on younger men who distinguish themselves in dangerous enterprises, but it is also sometimes given to those who have opposed or differed from him. It must be admitted also that he lacks one of the distinguishing characteristics of great men—ingratitude. He is always most generous—sometimes too generous —in his praise of the aides and assistants most closely associated with him in the two world wars.

These estimates of character and achievement have always been one of Sir Winston's favourite topics and in *Great Contemporaries* he wrote a number of brilliant sketches of some of the great figures of his time who had passed away. They are entirely free from party rancour and, indeed, Churchill has had so many labels that he easily escapes this danger. But though these essays in dissection show the skill of a master's hand, Churchill is even better at revealing by striking descriptions of particular incidents the character of those with whom he has worked in the course of his career.

His delineation of Stanley Baldwin and Neville Chamberlain has probably determined their place in history for all time. No doubt his judgments on the admirals and generals whom he directed in two world wars will often have to be corrected when all the evidence is available. His estimate of the contribution of Admirals Jellicoe and Beatty for example has by no means had universal acceptance. There will undoubtedly be similar revisions when the military events of the last war are better known and the point of view of the commanders themselves is more fully stated and appraised. But these judgments on those who were commanding the armies, navies, and airfleets are a great contribution to our understanding of the two world wars. They are written with such candour and fortified with such argument that they will make an indelible impression on the history of our time. No doubt also no one is more aware than Sir Winston himself that in passing judgment on others he has also made a major contribution to the judgment which history will pass upon him.

He is at his best when summing up his own countrymen and Americans. He is not so good at other nationalities. Though he became a great 'European' there is nothing cosmopolitan in his character and he has never had the opportunity of soaking himself in European countries as he has in the English-speaking world, India, and Africa. His Frenchmen, with the exception of Clemenceau, do not come alive in the same way as the British or Americans. There is, however, one great exception. For surely no one else succeeded so well in turning Generalissimo Stalin into a human being. Sir Winston had, indeed, exceptional opportunities for observation. But how well he availed himself of them! This is not to say that he solved the enigma, but at least we were shown something of the man behind the mask. President Roosevelt on the other hand is revealed mainly by his correspondence and by vivid description of his externals and entourage. He is treated with respect and affection. It could hardly be otherwise and other pens have not been slow to dwell on other aspects of the great President who supported us at the crisis of our fate. On the other hand President Wilson, with whom Churchill had not, of course, the same intimate relations, is treated much less sympathetically in *The World Crisis*. He is surprisingly antipathetic to one who, with all his defects, alone made possible the great experiment in international organization to which in later years Churchill himself was to attach such high importance. No doubt others would disagree violently with other appreciations. But, whatever reservations are made, Churchill has produced an imperishable gallery of portraits of the great personalities of his age as satisfying and instructive as those of Reynolds and Gainsborough and certainly painted with less flattery than those in the Waterloo Chamber at Windsor Castle.

But this aspect is, after all, less important than the narrative of events in which the portraits are set. In the chronicles of the two world wars this is supported by his own unrivalled documentation. In his prefaces Churchill repeats again and again that he is telling the story as seen by himself at the time, that it has always been his habit to record all action in writing and that he is thus able to substantiate what he now writes with indisputable contemporary evidence. This promise is amply fulfilled by the minutes, memoranda, letters, and cables which he places before his readers. And since it has ever been his purpose in these communications to combine cogency, clarity, and stimulus, they nearly always make excellent reading.

Much of this material is placed in the appendices, especially in *The Second World War*, but many documents appear in the text itself and it might be thought that the flow of the narrative is too much interrupted by them. This, however, is rarely the case. The later observations on the contemporary documents are always most skilfully inserted and the reader feels as if the papers were being handed to him to read accompanied by a confidential commentary by their author. Churchill seems to admit us to the most intimate thoughts and emotions which he himself experienced during the course of the events which he describes. This is one reason why the books have had so wide an appeal to all kinds of readers. We share to the full the anxieties, the triumphs, the defeats and even the humiliations of the author. We enter, as it were, the Admiralty, No. 10 Downing Street, the villas at Casablanca and Teheran, and sit down with the statesmen and their military advisers as they confer, debate, and wrangle and finally make the decisions which determine the course of history. No other author of such eminence, so far as I am aware, possesses this same gift to the same degree as Sir Winston Churchill.

The secret history of the two great wars has thus been revealed almost immediately after their conclusion to a degree never allowed in any previous generation, and Churchill has given us papers from his own archives as secret and intimate as any that have been published elsewhere. Had he not been able to do so, the impression he produces would have been less overwhelming. A contemporary document is far more convincing than any asseveration or argument, however weighty or skilfully contrived. No one, I think, has ventured to criticize this frankness which affects the reputations of many others still alive and some with their careers still in the hazard. The chronicle of the Second World War is the report of the great leader to the generation which served under him. It is surely right in this democratic age that all should be allowed to learn secrets which would only have been known to a select few in previous generations. Had Churchill not published such documents much that is inaccurate and unfair in accounts produced in other countries would have been able to mislead and confuse public opinion. An obvious corollary follows. The same licence must be allowed to others, and those engaged in writing the war histories must be given the opportunity to use the secret documents with the same candour and regard for truth which Sir Winston himself has shown.

It must be remembered also that, though the documents are contemporary, the narrative has been written after a considerable interval of time in which the results of the actions have become known. The papers are also a selection, one no doubt made in good faith, but inevitably reflecting the subsequent course of history. No one has been more frank in admitting error than Churchill. But naturally these admissions are accompanied by explanations and these must be coloured by the lapse of time. No man can remember accurately the process of reasoning that led him over a long period of time to certain decisions unless he records it day by day in a document meant only for his own personal perusal. In some cases this has been done by men of action in a diary.

Churchill recorded his decisions and the arguments used to convince others in his minutes, letters, and other written documents but he did not keep a diary. Captain Harry C. Butcher, the personal aide and assistant of General Eisenhower, who accompanied him throughout his career as Commander-in-Chief, did keep one and in it he recorded, with much other private and intimate conversation, Churchill's opinion of diaries: 'The Prime Minister said,' he wrote, 'that it was foolish to keep a day-by-day diary because it would simply reflect the change of opinion or decision of the writer, which, when and if published, makes one appear indecisive and foolish. He cited the diary of a British general who had written in his diary one day, "There will be no war." On the next day war was declared. The diary was published posthumously and, consequently, the general was made to appear foolish. For his part, the Prime Minister said, he would much prefer to wait until the war is over and then write impressions, so that, if necessary, he could correct or bury his mistakes.'[1]

I am sure that this is a misleading account of the conversation. Captain Butcher does not seem at all to be aware, as, indeed, none of the Americans ever appear to be aware, that Churchill had already written a chronicle of the First World War. In this, so far from burying his mistakes, he had disclosed and discussed them. But it is, of course, true that minutes and memoranda written to instruct or convince others do not necessarily reveal all the mind of the writer as is sometimes done in an intimate diary, while there must be in the archives communications to and from Sir Winston which will modify or correct some of the impressions

---

[1] Captain Harry C. Butcher, U.S.N.R., *My three years with Eisenhower*, p. 270 (Eng. Edn.).

derived from the papers which he has himself selected. But, however this may be, we are given most intimate records of events not ten years old and the conviction remains, that while some things must necessarily be concealed, or at least veiled, after so short an interval of time, we possess an authentic account of the author's part in two world wars, while the whole series of events is illuminated and made comprehensible by the descriptions which he gives of the actions of others and the estimates he makes of their wisdom and folly.

But, however rigorous the selection, Churchill's own papers, the papers of others, the revelations of the enemy archives, and the huge quantity of indispensable official records of the two world wars, presented a mass of material which no man could have surveyed, analysed, and transformed into a vivid narrative without the assistance of others. In this matter also Churchill has shown himself more skilful than other chroniclers. Eminent men who write books nearly always use others to help them, secretaries, research assistants, and collaborators. Too often, they have employed 'ghosts' and assumed the responsibility for thoughts and words which could never have come from their own minds or pens. Some eminent American contributors to the history of the Second World War have taken the better course of frankly avowing that the book has been written by another working with them and under their supervision. But such a narrative does not express a man's personality in the same way as if it had been written by himself. Sir Winston Churchill has adopted other methods. The contributions of his collaborators have been part of the raw material of the book, not the book itself. He has in a remarkable degree the facility of using their assistance and advice for his own purposes while reserving to himself the task of conveying to his readers the results of their collaboration. In *The River War* he had the assistance of an editor who no doubt saved him from many factual errors in a book executed at such speed. He had also the wisdom to submit his account of the history of the occupation to no less a person than Sir Evelyn Baring himself, who, after a momentary hesitation, was not slow to seize the opportunity. 'It is very much better,' reflected Mr. Churchill thirty years later, 'to have one's weak points indicated by friendly critics before one acts, rather than by hostile critics when it is too late to alter.'[1] As he rose in eminence he was able to surround himself with able and devoted helpers. His power to command such service, always exacting because of his own energy and imagination, was one of the secrets of his success. He had thus available men whom he could fully trust to assist him when his war chronicles were written. In addition, he always had at his disposal a larger circle of experts of every kind who could supply him with information, advice, or even criticism. His administrative ability and power of writing enabled him to absorb all they could do easily enough and impress his personality on the whole book, nearly all of which is clearly written or dictated by himself. Occasionally, it is true, a passage appears which would seem to owe a good deal to another hand. But these are rare and the discriminating use of experts is no doubt one reason why so few misstatements of fact have been found in the large expanse of Sir Win-

[1] *My Early Life*, p. 229.

ston's chronicles. We live in an age in which much history is syndicated and often loses not only its flavour but its form and texture in the process. Churchill's chronicles remain always his own personal contribution to the history of our time.

It is true, also, that Churchill is at his best when he describes events in which he himself played a determining role. He is naturally not so successful in interesting the reader in those which he has only surveyed from afar. Thus the book on the Eastern Front in *The World Crisis*, though often penetrating and illuminating, is below the level of interest of the previous volumes, while his account of the peace-making in *The Aftermath* suffers from the fact that he was then on the periphery of power and took only a small part in making the great decisions of the Conference. Similarly, his descriptions of the conflict in the Pacific in *The Second World War* are little more than summaries of other people's writings. He does not possess, or at any rate reveal, any special insight into the remarkable strategic problems of that area. These summaries serve as a background to the account of his own influence on the tragedy of Singapore and the fighting on the Burma front.

These experiences of adversity are discussed with great frankness and more than once in his chronicle of the last war Churchill pauses to reflect on the possibility of his own fall from power as a result of the defeats of our armies in the field. He is, indeed, in all his writings always a philosopher as well as chronicler, giving us not the philosophy of the schools but one which he has made for himself out of his great experience of active life. He constantly dwells upon the transience of human power and glory and is always conscious of the dangers of victory and the consolations of defeat. He continually reminds his readers of the part played in human affairs by what he terms luck or fortune or fate. He has himself experienced great reverses of fortune and has had more than once to watch others inadequately filling the place of which he himself has been deprived. 'One must never forget when misfortunes come,' he wrote when reviewing his own early life, 'that it is quite possible they are saving one from something much worse; or that when you make some great mistake, it may very easily serve you better than the best-advised decision. Life is a whole, and luck is a whole, and no part of them can be separated from the rest.'[1]

This habit of reflection was, indeed, innate and occurs in his earliest works. George Stevens, the most distinguished of Churchill's fellow war correspondents, to whom the manuscript of *The River War* was submitted, wrote: 'The only criticism I should make is that your philosophic reflections, while generally well expressed, often acute and sometimes true, are too devilish frequent.' This advice was taken in good part, but fortunately many reflections on life and death and human frailty remain and give to the book an atmosphere and appeal that would be lacking if they were absent. The young author even muses on the impermanence of his own contributions to history in a striking passage:

Each generation exults in the immediate pos-

[1] *My Early Life*, p. 116.

session of life, and regards with indifference, scarcely tinged by pride or pity, the records and monuments of those that are no more. The greatest events of history are insignificant beside the bill of fare. The greatest men that ever lived serve to pass an idle hour. The tremendous crash of the Roman Empire is scarcely heard outside the schools and colleges. The past is insulted as much by what is remembered as by what is altogether forgotten.[1]

Sir Winston Churchill has modestly called his surveys of the two world wars 'a contribution to history'. No doubt succeeding generations will be more interested in their own problems and struggles which may be even greater than those of our own time. But it is hard to believe that in this country at any rate, men and women will not return again and again to these splendid chronicles which record in language suited to the magnitude of their theme one of the greatest periods in our history, or that Sir Winston's own story will ever be surpassed in interest and importance by the multitude of other accounts that will follow it.

Charles K. Webster

[1] *The River War*, Vol. I, p. 11.

K

The Artist

by Sir John Rothenstein

'To know a painter,' said Delacroix after a visit to Corot, 'you must see him in his studio.' It was on 21 February 1949 that I was first accorded the privilege of thus visiting Sir Winston Churchill.

When I arrived at Chartwell no car stood in front of the house, and from the hall no sound was to be heard. Upon a table reposed an object familiar from innumerable photographs: a wide-brimmed, grey painting hat. I was contemplating this celebrated object with respect, as though it were the hat of a king sent to represent him on some ceremonial occasion, when I heard soft padding steps approach, and presently, dressed in his sky-blue siren-suit and shod in soft black slippers on which his initials were worked in gold, there appeared my host benignly welcoming.

Before lunch we visited his studio, a long narrow room brightly lit by high windows along two walls. Upon a long narrow table standing lengthwise to the room were ranged tidy rows of paint-tubes; beside it was the great terrestrial globe, a present, he told me, from the American Army. But for this globe, there was throughout the whole house a conspicuous absence of any display of trophies, historic battle orders and the like. The suggestion was made some years ago that Chartwell should one day be preserved as a museum. If it were left in its present state there would be little to remind the visitor of the fabulous career of its former owner, and filled with trophies it would give a false impression of his manner of living.

During our first visit to his studio Churchill told me that he would be grateful for any criticism of his painting I might care to make. 'Speak, I pray, with absolute frankness,' he urged as we went to lunch. As soon as we sat down he began to speak of Sickert: 'He came to stay here and in a fortnight he imparted to me all his considered wisdom about painting. He had a room specially darkened to work in, but I wasn't an apt pupil, for I rejoice in the highest lights and the brightest colours.' He spoke with appreciation of Sickert's knowledge of music halls, and he sang a nineteenth-century ballad he had learnt from him; and he sang it from beginning to end. 'I think the person who taught me most about painting was William Nicholson. I noticed you looking, I thought with admiration, at the drawings upstairs he made of my beloved cat.' During lunch his most memorable remark did not concern painters or painting. Upon his inquiring why I declined his offer of a cigar, I replied that every man should possess one virtue; the only one I could certainly claim was that I did not smoke: to which he instantly rejoined, 'There is no such thing as a negative virtue. If I have been of any service to my fellow men, it has never been by self-repression, but always by self-expression.' Back in the studio, fortified by a bottle of champagne, his invitation to give my opinion of his work without reserve seemed to me less alarming. In the course of the afternoon we must have looked at every one of the numerous paintings in the studio and the few that hung in various other parts of the house.

Churchill was so genial and so exhilarating a companion that before I had been with him long the notion of speaking with absolute frankness seemed as natural as it had earlier seemed temerarious. My first detailed criticism of one of his paintings had an unexpected, indeed a startling, result. About one of his landscapes— a wood on the margin of a lake—I offered the opinion that the shore was far too shallow, too lightly modelled and far too pale in tone to support the weight of the heavy trees with their dense, dark foliage, so that, instead of growing up out of the earth, they weighed it down. 'Oh,' he said, 'I can put that right at once; it would take less than a quarter of an hour,' and he began to look out the appropriate brushes and colours. 'But this painting, surely,' I said, 'must be among your earliest?' 'I did it about twenty years ago,' he conceded. 'Well then,' I protested, 'surely it's impossible for you to recapture the mood in which you painted it, or indeed your whole outlook of those days.' 'You really are convinced of that,' he grumbled, abandoning the notion of repainting with evident reluctance. This was the first of several occasions when I had to persuade him to desist from repainting an early work in consequence of some criticism of mine. 'If it weren't for painting,' Sir Winston said as we left the studio, 'I couldn't live; I couldn't bear the strain of things.'

The key to the understanding of Churchill's own painting is to be found, I believe, in a few sentences in his essay, *Painting as a Pastime*. These explain the seeming contradiction between the known personality and experience of the painter, and the character of the work; between the man profoundly and consistently preoccupied with the affairs of men, above all in their political and military aspects, and the small landscapes in which there is nowhere any intimation of struggle or tragedy, and in which, indeed, man scarcely figures at all. To many his little, gay, brilliantly coloured canvases seem to bear no relation to their creator, but such people make insufficient allowance for the difficulties of the art of painting. Had the fairies stuck a paint brush into his hand instead of a pen into one and a sword into the other, had he learnt while still a boy to draw and to paint, had he dedicated an entire laborious lifetime to the tempering of his powers, and to the disciplining of his visual imagination, these powers would have been immeasurably greater. Then he would have been equipped to express a large part of himself, instead of a few facets. He would have painted big pictures (it is significant that in his essay he calls pictures 'great' when the context shows that he means 'big'). There can be little doubt that he would have represented human beings and their affairs. In fact I recall his exclaiming, on an earlier occasion when we were looking at 'Napoleon on the *Bellerophon*', 'I don't see why artists to-day regard great themes as less legitimate than trivial ones.' Fully equipped he would have been what in the age of Reynolds was called a 'history' painter. His circumstances were in fact quite different. He was a late starter; he had neither the systematic training nor the leisure necessary to develop his talents to the full. He does not undertake heroic themes, large organizations of figures in action—many figures, perhaps, in vigorous action— he does not undertake them because they demand what the circumstances of his public life have denied him, the most expert knowledge and a long daily experience of painting.

Sir Winston's consistent awareness of his limitations is implicit in the sentences which give the key to his work:

> The painter must choose between a rapid impression, fresh and warm and living, but probably deserving only of a short life, and the cold, profound, intense effort of memory, knowledge, and will-power, prolonged perhaps for weeks, from which a masterpiece can alone result. It is much better not to fret too much about the latter. Leave to the masters of art trained by a lifetime of devotion the wonderful process of picture-building and picture-creation. Go out into the sunlight and be happy with what you see.

This awareness led him to cultivate the possibilities open to him with the utmost assiduity and resource. He is therefore able to do much more than enjoy himself in the sunlight. The skilful choice of subjects within his range to which he can respond ardently enables him to paint pictures that convey and enhance delight and are distinguished by their painterly qualities, pictures, too, that have an intimate and direct relation to his outlook on life. In these there comes surging irrepressibly up his sheer joy in the simple beauties of nature: water, still, bubbling, or agitated by wind; snow immaculate and crisp; trees, dark with the density of their foliage or dappled by sunlight; fresh flowers; distant mountains, and, above all, sunlight at its fiercest. The high peaks of his achievement, in my opinion, are 'The Goldfish Pool at Chartwell' (1948), 'The Loup River Quebec' (1947), 'Chartwell under Snow' (1947), and 'Cannes Harbour, Evening' (1923). These express, with insight and candour, his exultant enjoyment of living. 'I look forward,' he said, 'to a leisure hour with pleasurable agitation: it's so difficult to choose between writing, reading, painting, bricklaying, and three or four other things I want to do.'

It is relevant, in view of a deliberate attempt to associate the illustrious name of Sir Winston with vulgar attacks upon Picasso, Matisse, and other contemporary painters outside the academic fold, to point out that not only does he himself belong to what is likely to be the last phase of Impressionism, but that the expressive violence of the colour in his later pictures shows that he has looked with sympathy at Post-Impressionism as well. The evidence of his painting is reinforced by that of his written tribute to his masters. 'But surely,' he wrote in his essay, 'we owe a debt to those who have so wonderfully vivified, brightened, and illuminated modern landscape painting. Have not Manet and Monet, Cézanne and Matisse, rendered to painting something of the same service which Keats and Shelley gave to poetry after the solemn and ceremonious perfections of the eighteenth century? They have brought back to the pictorial art a new draught of *joie de vivre*; and the beauty of their work is instinct with gaiety, and floats in sparkling air.'

The Sportsman

by H. H. THE AGA KHAN

IT is now fifty-seven years since I first came to know
our present Prime Minister, Sir Winston Churchill, and
I am happy to recall that on that occasion it was with
regard to race-horses.

The late Lord Randolph Churchill had considerable
success as a race-horse owner and, when one takes into
consideration the number of important owners and
breeders that patronized the turf in the eighties and
nineties of the last century, Lord Randolph's success
was most remarkable. He won the Oaks with a mare
called l'Abbesse de Jouarre and I have been told by men
like Lord Marcus Beresford and Lord William Beresford that Lord Randolph was an exceptionally good
judge not only of men but of horses. The late Lady
Randolph Churchill, whom I had the honour of knowing quite well, and who was always a kind and good
friend of mine, often spoke to me of the keen interest
that Lord Randolph took in racing. Thus it may be said
that the Prime Minister was brought up in an atmosphere, not only of Parliament and statesmanship but
of the turf as well.

One fine morning at the height of the season (in August or September 1896) in Poona, I was informed by the then Governor of Bombay, Lord Sandhurst, that several officers of the 4th Hussars, who were then staying with him at Government House, would like to see my horses and stables. In those days I had the best race-horses in Western India. Though at the time I was too ill myself to show them round, these officers were shown all our horses by one of my cousins. One of the visitors, perhaps the most keenly interested of all, was our present Prime Minister.

I met the Prime Minister later in 1902, staying as a guest of Lord and Lady Warwick at Warwick Castle, when I was myself one of the house party. We had many discussions as to the comparative merits of polo and hunting, Sir Winston standing for polo while I, as a regular follower of hounds after jackals in India, championed hunting. Sir Winston's success as a polo player was all the more extraordinary owing to the fact that polo is a jealous mistress and those who have been most successful have given the greater part of their time and attention to this difficult and dangerous but beautiful sport. Winston Churchill was a regular player of polo, even when a member of the 1906 Liberal Government, and an active one throughout the time he was in the 1900 Parliament. His relative and friend, Mr. Freddy Guest (a great friend of mine who stayed a great deal with me in Calcutta over long periods), often told me that if he had given more time and attention to polo, he would certainly have been one of its champions.

During the house party at Warwick Castle, one day

at lunch Churchill surprised us all by reciting the names of the last fifty Derby winners and their breeding; an extraordinary exhibition of memory but one that goes a long way to prove that what he must have heard of in his early years at the parental home had not been forgotten.

Everyone connected with it, whether as owner, breeder, trainer, jockey, vet, or stable lad is, I know, proud and happy that in the midst of his many cares and enormous responsibilities, the Prime Minister has found time to patronize the turf.

We all heard with joy, when he first announced it, the news that he had bought some young horses and everybody hoped that what is known as beginner's luck might come his way, but little did we think that the modest Colonist would turn out to be one of the most remarkable and successful of modern purchases. Sir Winston nearly won the Gold Cup, beating all the French and English champions except one. His other victories are well known to those interested in the turf; it shows remarkable judgment on the part of the Prime Minister, almost uncanny judgment, to have picked up Colonist. Breeding a Derby winner entails the exercise of considerable judgment concerning the possible combination of blood that can make a horse of this quality, and this gives an advantage to the students of bloodstock history. But picking up a horse with few credentials like Colonist and bringing him to Ascot to beat nearly the whole field in the greatest long-distance race in the world needs exceptional judgment. Sir Winston's other purchases, too, have been extremely wise considering the prices paid by him. The trainer of Colonist told a friend of mine that Sir Winston's judgment in deciding the objectives for each horse and adjusting its racing career to its capabilities shows an insight that only one who from early life had taken an interest in the turf could be capable of.

I myself am ready to pay still greater compliments to the Prime Minister's judgment. I am convinced that the Colonists will be an acquisition of importance to breeders in Great Britain and this will bring a new element which, directly or indirectly, will enrich the English race-horse.

Aga Khan

Winston Churchill—as I Know Him

by LADY VIOLET BONHAM CARTER

I COUNT myself blessed to be able to write after his name the words 'as I know him'.

The stock question: 'What Great Man in history would you most like to have known?' presents no problem to me. I have my answer ready. While others hesitate and haver between Julius Cæsar, Sir Isaac Newton, Alexander, and Napoleon, I tell myself and them that they can have the lot. Because I do know Winston Churchill. And however high or low one may assess his place in history, his service to mankind, the English-speaking world, the British Commonwealth, and other substantial entities, I am convinced that as a man to know he can put most of the Great Shades in the shade.

But though he may be the best Great Man to know, he is the most difficult man to write about—because he has written better of himself than anyone can ever write about him. If, to quote his own words, 'there is little in that field unploughed', it is because the Master-

Ploughman has already furrowed it. Anything others write about him must inevitably be a pale paraphrase of the story he has written so incomparably about himself—sometimes as a straight narrative, sometimes woven like a gleaming thread into the pattern of the vast events he helped to shape.

He has a rare self-knowledge. Many know others better than they know themselves. Winston Churchill knows himself better than he knows other people. He has a liking, even a warm affection for himself, but no illusion. Of arrogance he might well be accused, but never of vanity.

I remember vividly the first time I 'saw him plain'. It was at a dinner party to which I went as a very young girl. He, with his dramatic South African exploits behind him and a political career in the making, was already on the high road to fame. His critics might have called it notoriety. For then, as always, he had critics. His unabashed confidence, unsquashable resilience, his push and dash and flair for taking short cuts through life, his contempt for humdrum conformity, have always challenged stuffy, stolid, stick-in-the-mud opinion here and elsewhere. No one knows better how to perform the public service known as 'putting the cat among the pigeons'.

I found myself sitting next to this young man who seemed to me quite different from any other young man I had ever met. For a long time he remained sunk in abstraction. Then he appeared to become suddenly aware of my existence. He turned on me a lowering gaze and asked me abruptly how old I was? I replied that I was nineteen. 'And I,' he said almost despairingly,

'am thirty-three already. Curse ruthless time! Curse
our mortality! How cruelly short is the allotted span
for all we must cram into it.' And he burst forth into an
eloquent diatribe on the shortness of human life and the
immensity of possible human accomplishment—a theme
so 'well-ploughed' by the poets, prophets, and philo-
sophers of all ages that it might seem difficult to invest
it with a new and startling significance.

Yet for me he did so, in a torrent of magnificent
language which seemed both effortless and inexhaustible
and ended up with the words I shall always remember:
'We are all worms. But I do believe that I am a glow-
worm.' And there and then I felt a glow which had not
come my way before. I knew that I had 'seen a great
light'. I recognized it as the light of genius.

When I proclaimed to others my discovery I was
mocked by many. How, they asked, did I know a
genius when I saw one? Could I define a genius? How
could I recognize what I was unable to define? I might
(if I had known them at the time) have replied in Dr.
Johnson's words: 'We all know what light is, but it is
not easy to *tell* what it is.'

It is also possible to recognize that which we have
never known. As the water diviner knows when the
rod leaps in his hand that he is near a spring, something
is added to our vision which we could not have seen with
our own eyes—the irrational certainty which we call
revelation.

No book of Sir Winston Churchill's is more self-
revealing than his *Painting as a Pastime*. 'Be persuaded,'
he wrote, 'that the first quality that is needed is Auda-

city. There really is no time for the deliberate approach.'

How faithfully he has applied his own advice. 'Splash into the turpentine, wallop into the blue and white . . . then several large, fierce strokes and slashes on the absolutely cowering canvas.' Thus he approached life —though, unlike the canvas, life did occasionally hit back.

And in his life as in his painting he has always loved bright colours, 'rejoiced with the brilliant ones', and had little use for the 'poor browns'. Although in Heaven he hopes for a still gayer palette, on which orange and vermilion will be the 'darkest, dullest colours', he has made and is still making good use of both on earth. There is no twilight in his mind. He has lived under dark and dazzling skies, but he has never known one grey day.

I remember in his early painting days when we were both staying in a country house, set in a monochrome of dull, flat, uneventful country, I went out to watch him paint, half wondering what he would make of it. Looking over his shoulder I saw depicted on his canvas range upon range of mountains, rising dramatically behind the actual foreground. I searched the skies for a mirage and then inquired where they had come from—and he replied: 'Well—I couldn't leave it quite as dull as all that.' No landscape and no age in which he lived could ever be consigned to dullness. But in his own there was no need to snatch the brush out of the hands of Fate.

Sir Winston has rightly called his life 'A Roving Commission'. Reading his own account of its beginning in that enthralling book, *My Early Life*, and watching

the rest take place before my eyes, I sometimes thought
—until the last world war—that he had been born out
of due season, that he should rightly have belonged to
an age in which thought and action were a combined
operation instead of being as they are in these days,
alternative functions, each allotted to specialists in their
own sphere. 'After all,' he wrote regretfully, 'a man's
life must be nailed to a cross either of thought or action.'
The realm of thought alone has always seemed to him
to be an insufficient kingdom, cramping and cold.
Where his imagination soars, his body needs must
follow. If his mind is busy with war he must command
troops, if he argues with bricklayers he himself must
build a wall. Only the King's command prevented
him from taking part in the D-Day operations,
and had he done so from a ship he might well have
followed his heart on to the beaches. Sidney Street,
Antwerp, many of the incidents in his career which
have been most harshly criticized, have arisen from this
imperious need to combine thought with action, this
refusal to accept the ruling of the modern world that we
must either plan or perform, conceive or execute, but
that the machinery of Government is so ordered that it
is not permissible to do both. In this respect, during the
years of war when every decision was fraught with vital
action he entered into his double heritage.

Action is the key-note, the life-blood of his nature.
He has never known a fallow or a barren moment. In
times of political misfortune when the main current of
his life's stream was dammed, it broke its banks and
overflowed tumultuously into new channels. He painted
pictures, he constructed waterworks, he built miles of

L

brick wall, he wrote immortal books. 'I have noticed in my life,' he wrote, 'deep resemblances between many different kinds of things. Writing a book is not unlike building a house or planning a battle or painting a picture. The technique is different, the materials are different, but the principle is the same.'

Readers of his books will find in this reflection an explanation, almost a definition of their quality. In their structure and proportions they are architectural ('the foundations have to be laid, the data assembled and the premises must bear the weight of their conclusions'); colour is splashed about their pages with the brush of a master-painter; the writing is in itself a kind of action. We are swept forward on its surge and tide like a ship before a following wind. There is never a moment when either we or he himself are becalmed in his theme.

As words, thoughts, images pour from his pen we feel the impulse of a torrent whose source is inexhaustible. As I read I think often of Blake's proverb: 'The cistern contains—the fountain overflows.' Sir Winston is never the cistern, he is always the fountain. And as the fountain plays he writes—fulfilling a natural function.

Ever since early youth words have been his toys, his tools, the beloved children of his mind. He has told us how as a young Hussar of twenty-two at Bangalore he began to feel the urgent need to use them. 'I caught myself using a good many words the meaning of which I could not define precisely. I admired these words, but was afraid to use them for fear of being absurd.' Happily it did not take him long to exorcize this phobia.

It is interesting to reflect that in his mastery of

language he owes nothing to the classics. Indeed he has never hesitated to put them in their place. 'Those Greeks and Romans,' I have heard him say to my father, 'they are so overrated. I have said just as good things myself. They owe their reputation to the fact that they got in first with everything.' And my father's mild plea that they must be given at least a little credit for this, as the world had been going on for quite a long time before they appeared on the scene, went quite unheeded.

Whether Sir Winston's style would have gained or suffered from a classical education we can but guess. But not one of us can regret that he decided to dispense with it. His natural ear for the music of language needed no tuning-fork. He has said truly of himself that he 'has in his bones the essential structure of the ordinary British sentence which is a noble thing'. And though the arts of writing and of speaking are often mutually destructive, he is equally master of both.

DEMAGOGY

Words are the armoury of politics and power its prize. Yet though he loves power and has command of every verbal weapon, he has never been a demagogue.

He has never had his ear to the ground. Nor would he feel much interest in its message—even if he heard it. It is his own message which concerns him and which he is determined to transmit. The processes of his own powerful and self-sustaining mind are, not unnaturally, of far greater interest and moment to him than those of (what is called) 'the Common Man'.

Lord Keynes once compared Mr. Lloyd George to 'a prism which collects light and distorts it'. Sir Winston has never been a receptive and reflective prism. He has always been the light—powerful—intense—direct and concentrated as a beam.

During long periods of his life the British public, who are apt to mistrust brilliance and dislike a glare, just blinked and turned aside.

Until fourteen years ago he had no organized body of support behind him either in Parliament or in the country. Three months before the outbreak of war a letter advocating his inclusion in the Government was considered unfit for publication by *The Times*. He was left to rust unused on a back-bench.

We recall the well-worn clichés used about him in the past—'unstable'—'erratic'—'not a safe man'. Not safe enough perhaps to fill the arm-chair of a humdrum office in safe days—but when all was at stake, when our existence and the fate of civilization were rushing towards the rapids, we saw him in the lightning-flash of danger as the one man 'strong to save'.

It is interesting to consider why this revelation so suddenly accomplished had been so long delayed. In 1940 Churchill was sixty-six. He had been for forty years exposed to the fierce light of the political arena. How came it that a man who had never been the leader of any political party in the State was acclaimed by all as the unchallenged leader of the nation—its voice, its will, its soul?

Sir Winston himself gave one answer to this question when he said that 'to hold the leadership of a party or nation with dignity and authority requires that the leader's qualities and message shall meet not only the need but the mood of both'. Not only did he then meet the nation's need, but he became the inspired expression of its mood and purpose.

There are moments in the life of nations when those who lead them are unmasked by circumstance. Fate ruthlessly confronts men with a task beyond their powers and those who seemed great in small days in great days prove infinitely small. Just such a challenge of Fate at long last enabled Churchill's fellow-country-men to see him plain. The greatness of the hour revealed his own.

During the years of war he spoke to us in 'words that might create a soul under the ribs of death'. He created in each one of us his own heroic image of ourselves until we were transmuted by his faith into the people he believed in. We were that people—but we did not know it until he he had revealed us to ourselves. By the spell of his imagination, "which in truth is but another name for absolute power", war was invested with a splendour and significance in which its suffering and squalor were submerged.

Many of his speeches deserve to rank with those of the immortal orators of Greece and Rome and they will live as long. And yet to call them classics does not quite describe them, for his style combines a classic form and balance with a fire and colour which are his own alone. Each word bears his own signature—an autograph which would defy the forgery of ghosts and shadow-writers the world over. There lurks in every sentence the ambush of the unexpected. Yet he is not afraid of striking tonic major chords, of uttering truths so simple and eternal that on another's lips they would be truisms. By clothing them in his own words he reinstates them on their thrones.

One of the proofs of greatness is the power to learn from life, to go on growing to the end.

Coleridge once wrote that to most men 'experience is like the stern lights of a ship which illumine only the track it has passed'. To Sir Winston it has also been a searchlight showing the way ahead. He has grown steadily in patience, tolerance, and wisdom. When in our hour of direst need we were refused the right to use the Irish ports his forbearance touched a height of statesmanship of which in youth he might have fallen short. It is this power of growth which makes him (as Cicero said of Cæsar) incalculable.

Yet in his fundamental outlook he has shown throughout his life a rare consistency. In changing from one party to another he has never sacrificed a principle (except perhaps once—when as a member of Mr. Baldwin's Government he swallowed Tariffs). He has always followed his own lights and pursued his own aims, now in one combination, now in another, often alone.

Though a natural partisan, he has never been a party politician. In order to extend himself he needs a national, or better still, an international setting. He has never been the orthodox mouthpiece of the creed of any party. He could not squeeze himself into the strait-jacket of any ready-made doctrine. They were all misfits.

The Tory Party seemed his natural home. But despite his historic sense of tradition he is untrammelled by

convention. Despite his romantic feeling for the aris-
tocracy his broad humanity transcends the boundaries of
class. His intensely individual and adventurous mind,
forever on the move, could never be 'contained' by the
Conservatives and its questing, restless brilliance has
often filled them with an unconcealed disquiet.

The Liberals in their great days gave him more
scope and a better run. (To their credit they have
never been afraid of quality.) But though a democrat
to the bone, imbued with a deep reverence for Parliament and a strong sense of Human Rights, he was
never quite a Liberal. He never shared the reluctance
which inhibits Liberals from invoking force to solve a
problem.

And though he revels in discussion he is by temperament an intellectual autocrat. He does not like having
other people's way. He infinitely prefers his own.

If he has often been out of step with his contemporaries it is because he has so frequently seen further
ahead than they did. His perspective is historic in its
range and sweep. He 'looks before and after', relates
the immediate present to the far horizon, skipping the
molehills in the middle distance which to other eyes
seem mountains.

His warnings against the Nazi peril in the thirties,
his speech at Fulton urging the Free World to stand
together in unity and strength and meet the Communist challenge to our Christian civilization, his
appeal at Zurich to Europe to forgive old wrongs, unite
and save itself—all these great flashes of prophetic
vision were at the time either denounced, derided, or
ignored. Yet every one of them has since been vindi-

cated by events. His great speech to the House of Commons on 11 May 1953 proposing a meeting of the Great Powers was another instance of the immediacy and flexibility of his mind. Again he alarmed all those (and there are many) who prefer attitudes to action and who dare not take the risks of hope.

AS A MAN

Sir Winston Churchill is a theme on which no one could speak or write dispassionately. He provokes the extremes of feeling both as a statesman and a man. In his presence it would be impossible to be tepid, inert, or numb about anything whatsoever, but least of all about himself.

As a statesman he has inspired among all sorts and conditions of men and women in many lands a passionate allegiance. He is a living legend the world over. Among his political opponents at home he has aroused fury—bewilderment—exasperation—but seldom hatred and never indifference.

As a man he is not so much liked as loved. Fortune endowed him not only with a double charge of life, but with a double dose of human nature. He is a man and not a superman. His character spans the whole gamut of human possibilities—its frailty, foibles, grandeur, and nobility. He can be Puck and prophet, sage and wit, above the battle—in the scrum—an epic poet—and a tease. (What other Prime Minister in our history has ever kissed his hand to an almost apoplectic Opposition or put out his tongue at it?)

He can bear the world upon his shoulders. Yet he is

vulnerable to the simplest emotions and can find absorbing pleasure among goldfish, cats, and swans.

'I had been so happy in the nursery with my toys,' he once wrote of his childhood days. He is still happy with his toys, and daily adding to them for he has never ceased to be a child. It is characteristic of him that when Home Secretary he obdurately refused to prohibit roller-skating on the pavements. What did it matter if a few old women were knocked down? It was more important that little boys should not be disinherited of their fling of fun.

He loves the pride of life, pace, colour, exuberance, and hope. He shuns the drab, the neutral, the cautious, and the cocoa-blooded. His thought is never cold. It is incandescent with an ardour that quickens all it touches. He was once described by an acute observer as 'thinking with his heart'. It would be equally true to say of him that he feels with his mind.

More than most men he feels at home with friends and likes to work with them. He has always found personal intimacy a lubricant in business. It may even be that he tends to overrate those with whom he can communicate in his own code.

His friendship is a stronghold against which the gates of Hell cannot prevail and the absolute quality of his loyalty is fully known only to those who are safe within its walls. In a friend he will defend the indefensible, explain away the inexplicable—even forgive the unforgivable. Intolerant of criticism and opposition, he will accept both from those of whose affection he is assured—always providing that they are couched in the right idiom. Those who wish to gain his ear, hold his attention, reach his imagination, must bait their hook with the right words.

No one is easier to bore; nor does he seek to veil his boredom by any softening subterfuge. He has the disconcerting power to insulate himself at will from any company and brood remote in an impenetrable shell.

William James once wrote that men of genius differ from ordinary men, not in any innate quality of the brain, but in the aims and purposes on which they concentrate and in the degree of concentration which they manage to achieve. Sir Winston has a power of intellectual and emotional concentration amounting almost to obsession—and with it the uncanny knack of switching his undivided mind from one target to another.

To write the history of the Second World War would for most men have been a whole-time occupation demanding several years' seclusion in an ivory tower. He produced his masterpiece in the brief intervals of a fierce political struggle—first to gain power and then to use it.

I have had the supreme good fortune to know Winston Churchill. But from the day of our first meeting in my early youth I have seen him always in a dual perspective. Through and beyond my friend—well known and dearly loved—I see one of the greatest figures of all time upon the stage of history.

For me it would be vain to attempt to assess the elements that have gone to the making of this epic character—statesman—soldier—orator—writer—artist-in-action—and yet withal the most human of human beings.

In this age of prostrate masses when men drift helplessly upon the tide which we call 'history', his existence and achievement restore our faith in the power of Man to shape his own fate and the world's.

For in 1940 Winston Churchill did by himself turn the tide of history. His 'shoulders held the sky suspended'; he 'stood and Earth's foundations stay'. Never, in his own words, 'was so much owed by so many' to one single man. He saved his country and the cause of human freedom which is 'its message and its glory'. He defied Destiny and fulfilled his own. In his own life-time he has taken his place among the Immortals.

Violet Bonham Carter

A Birthday Letter

from BERNARD BARUCH

March 30, 1954

MY DEAR WINSTON:

Some men are fortunate enough to leave this world of printing presses, radio, and television before their chauffeurs and butlers, drinking and gin rummy companions can unloose their reminiscences of the great man's life to an audience avid for every detail. You are not to be spared this.

I don't know whether you object, although no word portrait that anyone could sketch of you could compare with the self-portrait you have drawn with your own writings and deeds. For my part, though, I do object to your eightieth birthday being used as an occasion for summing up your life. How can one sum up a life to which new achievements are still being added?

Towering as is your stature now, you may enhance it still more. So let us wait until the record is complete before we sum up. I myself write these pages for the pleasure of paying tribute to a dear friend who on his eightieth birthday remains a man of the future.

We have been friends for almost forty years now. For me, at least, that friendship has been like your garden at Chartwell, a source of inspiration and pleasure which has grown more rewarding with each passing year.

We first came to know each other before we had met. During World War I, when you were Britain's Minister of Munitions and I Chairman of the War Industries Board in the United States, we exchanged messages frequently. Most of these messages were of a routine nature which revealed little of your personal qualities. Then occurred two episodes which showed how diamond-like was your character—the greater the difficulties and frictions to which it was exposed, the more brilliantly it shone.

The first episode concerned nitrates from Chile, then the sole source for all the Allies. The United States negotiated an agreement to supply what Chile needed in return for all the nitrate she could produce. This agreement could have been used for commercial advantage—but that would have been contrary to the spirit in which we had associated ourselves with our allies.

And so an International Nitrate Executive was established to allocate the available nitrate. The success of this board served as a pattern for similar boards in World War II. You were responsible for its success. Indeed, you were the 'Nitrate King' of World War I.

My second glimpse into your character came when I sent some of my associates to London to straighten out difficulties that had arisen in purchasing various raw materials. Our proposal was that England should pay the same price as we did for anything bought in the

United States. Americans, in turn, should pay the same price as England did for anything purchased from within the Empire. Some of your merchant princes opposed the idea. But you supported it as the only fair way for allies to treat one another.

Finally, when the first war ended, we did meet in person—in Paris during the Peace Conference.

One day we were walking through the Bois de Boulogne, talking of the problems which burdened a world exhausted by war and groping for peace. Suddenly you broke your brisk stride, paused and, lifting your walking stick, pointed to the East. Your voice rumbled ominously:

'Russia! Russia! That's where the weather is coming from!'

Even then you could feel the building up of that 'cold front' of tyranny and totalitarianism which now chills every people who cherish liberty.

Another remark of yours in Paris in those days is unforgettable. You had flown across the Channel at the request of Lloyd George to discuss what measures should be taken if Germany refused to sign the peace treaty.

You received me in your hotel suite, while you were dressing. I spoke to you with strong feeling of the spirit of vengeance which had animated the French and British through the difficult peace negotiations. I went on to warn of the consequences of a peace settlement based on revenge rather than reason.

You stood before the mirror, adjusting your cravat. Then you turned and said quite simply: 'I was all for war. Now I am all for peace.'

I doubt whether any single sentence you have uttered characterizes you better. You know what war means. You also know the meaning of dishonour and subjugation. Confronted with the choice of one or the other, no man has been more ready to endure the grief and carnage of war rather than surrender liberty and honour. Despite this, you have never sought a peace of revenge.

Your place in history will be that of one of the greatest of war leaders. But historians should not forget that yours was a war leadership impassioned not by hatred but by the desire for peace, freedom, and honour.

Once we came to know each other, you visited me whenever you were in the States and I never missed spending a few days with you whenever I was in Europe. Sometimes you took me around the country to visit your friends or to see the sights. Once while visiting Portsmouth Naval Station with Sir Roger Keyes, I heard one sailor murmur: 'Good old Winnie. He got us better pay.'

More often we would sit in your home at Chartwell or walk through its grounds. One moment we might be talking of your farm or of horses, and the next of approaching war. You could pause in the midst of denouncing the treachery of princes to point to the side of your house and exclaim: 'Look at that beautiful vine with its lovely flowers! That is something man cannot do—he can never equal what nature has done there.'

Some of those years were bleak ones for you, out of office and in disfavour even in your own Party. Once as we walked through your rose garden you unburdened yourself. Your public career seemed to have come to a dead end and you wondered whether you should not enter some business. I heartened you by pointing out that even if you were denied political leadership for a time, you could still achieve greatness with your pen. I felt certain that England would not and could not ignore you.

Those were the days in which you stood almost alone in England, warning of the danger of approaching war. Time and again you warned of the mounting strength of Hitler's legions and of the weaknesses of the nations he was planning to attack. But the public seemed to think that war could be prevented if only the world wished hard enough. I know how keenly you felt the accusation of 'warmonger' that was hurled at you, for that was the epithet pinned upon me in the United States for urging greater preparedness.

In the summer of 1938—the summer of Munich— I visited you. President Roosevelt had asked me to learn what I could of German airplane production and British and French 'rearmament'. You helped me make contact with the British experts. The day I left you remarked: 'Well, Bernie, the big war is coming. You will be in the forefront in America while I will be on the sidelines here.'

Fortunately, your reputation for far-sightedness does not rest upon that prediction.

The war brought you to the pinnacle of fame. It also forged new ties of understanding between you and America. Despite your single-minded devotion to Britain, you know America as do few other world leaders.

You have disagreed with our leaders and our policies from time to time. You have championed England's cause in every place and at every time but never for the purpose of thwarting or unfairly burdening America. I have heard you tell Franklin Roosevelt flatly during the war when the United States was faced with diverting supplies from Britain: 'My people are living at the limit of austerity now, and their food supplies cannot be cut.' And I have seen you protest as warmly against slurs upon America and her leaders as you would upon your own.

Once before the war you gave me a dinner. The only other Americans present were Admiral Cary Grayson and Senator Carter Glass. Among the other guests were several Tories of the old school who were hostile to Franklin Roosevelt and his New Deal. One such gentleman sought to amuse the company by asking me the riddle—why Roosevelt and Columbus were alike? The answer was that like Columbus, Roosevelt did not know where he was going or where he was when he got there, nor where he had been when he got back.

Neither you nor I were amused by this riddle. When I replied that there were other resemblances between Roosevelt and Columbus, that both had opened new frontiers and had explored new horizons, that both had provided new opportunities for the old world—you banged the table in approbation, with an enthusiastic 'Hear Hear!'

Almost every aspect of your life has been written of in exhaustive detail. One which has not received the consideration it merits is your conduct as an ally. All our futures hinge upon our abilities to hold together the alliance of free peoples. All of us could profit from the model you have set in your dealings with the United States. We have come to respect your devotion to your own country, knowing that it has not made you less understanding of other nations.

In the matter of the international control of atomic energy, for example, you, who know America so well, often expressed yourself on how fortunate it was for the cause of peace that the atomic bomb was in the possession of America. In the years ahead we must continue to try to find some means of bringing atomic energy under safe and sure control. The perspective you have shown will be a valuable example for those who might misunderstand American motives or be tempted to deceive themselves by accepting some meaningless 'agreement' which would only expose the nations who kept their word to atomic destruction.

As a proud descendant of a proud people, I know how unhappy it made you to have to seek financial aid from any source. But you have never been small in acknowledging the aid America has given Britain. As I have often assured you, most of us in the United States have been equally appreciative of Britain's role in the last war and since.

We have not always agreed. But, like a true friend, you have always borne with my contrary views. I can see you now, sunk down in your chair, listening to my heated arguments and murmuring: 'Now, Bernie dear.'

The world has seen you under the spotlight of world affairs. It knows you for your courage, for the strength of your leadership, for the force of your writings. But it knows little of Churchill in private life, the friend, husband, father, the gentle—even tender—side of you.

I wish the world could see you for a few moments, walking with your dog, Rufus, about your garden, marvelling at the beauty of a rose, or lecturing the fish in your pond as you feed them. The world should read the cables I have received from this master of English prose, when you were pleased with certain events, which read merely: 'Oh Boy.' Above all, the world should be a guest at your dinner table and enjoy the treat of hearing you talk, with a bottle of wine always at hand, of military tactics in the American Civil War, of your early adventures in South Africa, of Gibbon and Macaulay, of the knaves and fools you have known. The spirit with which you could denounce them!

There is also a quiet side to your life, of which the world should know, and which is perhaps best symbolized in your gracious and beautiful wife. No one but you knows how enormous has been Clemmie's influence and contribution to your own career. I have sensed your respect and devotion to her in how quickly you would heed her gentle admonition: 'Winston, I wouldn't say that.'

Some years ago, we were sitting in my house in New York City, playing gin rummy. Outside there was a parade in honour of Greek independence. The strains of martial music and the sound of marching feet sifted up even to our deaf ears. We went to the window and looked down on the ranks of marchers and the fluttering flags. You turned to me with sparkling eyes and, in a voice deep with emotion, said:

'You see, Bernie. They cannot quench freedom.'

They cannot indeed, Winston, as long as the world breeds men like you, who can call forth all of the best in humankind.

Happy Birthday—and many more birthdays to come.

Bernie

Epilogue

by THE RT. HON. ANTHONY EDEN

A COLLECTION of essays, each by a different writer, exemplifies better than any other method the diversity of Winston Churchill.

He is sometimes portrayed as belonging to another century. If this be the century of the Common Man, then that is certainly true; for he is no common man. The ideal of the complete man can have found no better realization even at the height of its popularity. A prodigious vitality has enabled him to be in turn soldier, statesman, historian, artist and sportsman with complete abandon and a perfect professionalism. Here is a lesson for this age of specialization. While relishing the glories of the past, he is too good an historian to disparage his own times, too full of zest to despair of the future.

It is, of course, Churchill's political life which I have known best. Open-mindedness is the secret of happiness and of a wise old age. During the seventeen years that he and I have worked together in politics this is one of the qualities that has impressed me most in him.

Churchill will never accept the orthodox objections to any course. He will continue to probe at a problem until it gives up its core. No man holds stronger opinions than he does, yet no one, given good advice to the contrary, is so likely to take it and to see the other point of view, even if the process of digestion be long.

He combines an instinctive perception with a strong will. He is therefore happiest and at his best when he feels something deeply and can reason powerfully for what he feels is right. This is just what happened in 1940. Then he expressed the instinctive conviction of the British people that they could not be beaten, and he gave them the leadership that made victory possible.

That is why, despite the wide range of his achievements, he could never be greater than in 1940, because it was our finest hour and his.

Anthony Eden